MUMMY'S NOT SICK ANYMORE

MUMMY'S NOT SICK ANYMORE

How Ali Watson fought cancer with faith, family and friends

NOEL DAVIDSON

AMBASSADOR INTERNATIONAL
GREENVILLE, SOUTH CAROLINA & BELFAST, NORTHERN IRELAND

www.ambassador-international.com

Mummy's Not Sick Anymore

How Ali Watson fought cancer with faith, family and friends.

ISBN: 978-1-935507-42-0

Page Design & Printed by Bethel Solutions
Cover Design Michael Holmes

Ambassador International
Emerald House
427 Wade Hampton Blvd
Greenville, SC 29609, USA

Ambassador Books and Media
The Mount
2 Woodstock Link
Belfast, BT6 8DD, Northern Ireland, UK

www.ambassador-international.com

The colophon is a trademark of Ambassador

Proceeds from the sale of this book are being donated to support the work of the Northern Ireland Hospice and Glenabbey Church.

Contents

FOREWORD

This is a story of life: of work and travel, of two people meeting and falling in love, of simple joys and pleasures, of hopes and plans for the future, of the arrival of two lively boys; of a diagnosis that changed everything and of a young woman's struggle to find God in the confusion and pain. You have it in your hands not because Alison Watson was a celebrity, but because the issue of her life is the issue of all our lives and she has something to say.

I had the privilege of knowing Alison and particularly of knowing her in the final months of her life as she invited me into the hard places of her journey. One long, profound and very direct conversation in the City Hospital has remained with me – the kind of conversation that is probably only possible for someone who knows she is dying. It was marked throughout by the refreshing yet heartbreaking honesty of a young woman struggling to come to terms with an increasingly bleak prognosis, her boys' future, a husband left behind and so many desires and expectations unfulfilled. She had reached the place where platitudes are an insult to pain and intelligence, where sentimental religious clichés are as welcome as sour milk. The wishful thinking and misplaced hopes in which many take refuge were utterly absent. In its place a growing faith.

Doubt is not the same as unbelief. It can, of course, lead to it. But it can also lead to deepening faith and on the way help blow away the deceptive mists of wishful thinking and false hopes and reveal solid ground.

Alison found that solid ground. She came to trust not simply in the love of God but also in his sovereign wisdom. She wrote in her journal that faith "is the only option." By this she did not mean faith in her own ability to believe. She meant faith in God himself. Which meant questions, yes, and discussion, even argument and tears but ultimately rest. She turned again to what God had said in his own words and found strength and comfort there, and liberation in her final days to receive and enjoy every evidence of grace that lined her way and strengthened her heart on her journey home. When God is all you have she discovered that God is all you need.

It is possible that you will finish the reading of this moving story with an admiring, if unspoken, "if only". "If only I had faith like that..." As if faith were some kind of psychological condition some of us are blessed with and others must remain forever without. It isn't true. Faith is not wishful thinking or psychological conditioning. It is a response to a person. We cannot know everything. But we can know some things. We do not receive the answers to all our questions in this life. But there are some answers, and Alison found them.

Faith, of course, is not actually the only option. There is another: unbelief, and with it ultimate hopelessness and despair for if we remove God we also remove all hope and all possibility of finding a meaning in our suffering. Alison knew this very well. But for her the evidence was too strong to discount: the reality of love, the meaningfulness of life and supremely Jesus – living among us, dying for us and rising on the other side of death. There was reason for hope.

I encourage you to read her story, follow her questions and discover the answers she found.

Gilbert Lennox,
Glenabbey Church   November 2010

INTRODUCTION

"A member of my staff has suggested you may be able to help me," a local Primary School Principal told me on the phone. "How do you mean?" I wanted to know. "Help in what way?" "Paul Watson, a friend from our church has just lost his wife, Alison," she explained. "Ali, as we called her, had cancer and during her illness she faced a lot of issues and recorded her thoughts and feelings in a journal. Paul feels that if her journal could be featured in a book it would help a lot of people."

It sounded like an interesting proposition, but initially I had my doubts.

Two things slightly concerned me. Firstly, could there be enough material in one handwritten journal to form the basis of a book? And again, was I the right person for the job? Had I sufficient experience of cancer care and spiritual struggle to write with the depth of understanding and tenderness of touch such subjects clearly demanded?

Then I met Paul, he introduced me to the journal, and I was hooked.

Paul was such a sincere Christian guy, just embarking on the challenge of bringing up two little boys, and some of the entries in that journal were so spiritually insightful, that I had to do something.

So I wrote a magazine article on Ali's illness, based around a series of quotes from her journal. This was published in Life Times in February 2009, with the understanding that we would reconsider the possibility of a book 'later in the year.'

A month later I was to gain the life experience I thought I lacked. In March '09 I was diagnosed with cancer and told I would require major surgery. This was performed in June and was followed by a period of physical weakness and spiritual questioning.

When hit with a number of complications following the operation, and feeling particularly 'down,' I began to wonder if God was hearing, not to mention answering, all the prayers that were being offered for me.

Paul got back to me in October to enquire if I had thought any more about 'the book idea,' and I let him know about my summer of trial. At that time I was still concentrating on regaining physical strength and spiritual confidence and wasn't really thinking ahead about anything.

By December, though, the whole outlook had changed. God had answered those prayers and I was making a remarkable recovery. My problem had been not so much a lack of prayer but a lack of patience.

Now I felt in some measure emotionally equipped to write about Ali and her journal. For more than half a year I had been allowed to paddle on the shore of the ocean of her experience. At least I knew what it was to have cancer, catheters and communion with God in a crisis.

I made contact with Paul again to find out if he was still interested.

Yes. Of course he was. In fact he and a friend had been praying two days earlier that God would guide me to be in touch!

We met just before Christmas and agreed a plan. Although Ali's sensitive and mostly spiritual journal entries would comprise the backbone of the story, there would be much more to it than that. We were about to embark on telling the story of someone who had poured out her innermost thought patterns on to paper. That was true, but this was also someone who had fought cancer, a person who was a loving wife and mother, devoted daughter, true friend, active church member and above all a woman of outstanding Christian faith.

The story unfolded over the following months of regular meetings. It begins with a love story, proceeds through a world tour to a wedding and the birth of two lovely little sons of whom mum and dad Watson were justly proud. That was the happy part, the early part.

Then Ali's mum was diagnosed with cancer and passed away.

Six months later Ali was to learn she had it too. She had treatment, thought she was cured but it came back. That was when she began writing it all down...

Her observations on topics as diverse as 'passing through the fire,' the possibility of healing, 'what's going to happen to my boys?' and 'the valley of the shadow of death,' moved me when I read them. When I quoted them in the book, often describing the circumstances in which they were written and sent a chapter or two to Paul he confessed at our next meeting, "I sat and cried when I read that. It brought it all back."

It's not all sad, though. There are lighter moments in the story reflecting Ali's great sense of humour. And there is a positive outcome.

Since Mark was able to tell his friends, "Mummy's not sick anymore," it has all been about Team Watson, with dad the coach and Mark and Euan, the sons, the star players. Paul has also become involved in fundraising for the Northern Ireland Hospice in appreciation of the excellent care his wife received during her stays there.

It has been an uplifting experience working with Paul on his project. We have laughed together, cried together, worked together and prayed together. I have been carried along on the wave of his enthusiasm and what we feel we have produced is an accurate and touching record of faith 'in the fire.'

Team Watson, the wider family circle and Paul's many friends at Glenabbey join Liz, my wife who is my constant source of support, and I in praying you may find this book moving, inspiring and challenging.

Above all it is our desire that it should bring glory to God, and cause you to examine the level, or existence, of your faith in Him. If you have a personal relationship with Jesus may you be encouraged in Him, and if you don't may you come to know Him as you read.

Noel Davidson   October 2010

CHAPTER 1
BY THE SEA

"I love being by the sea!" Paul Watson remarked for the third time without even realising it.

These involuntarily repeated observations amounted to more than a passing comment on favourable weather conditions and agreeable surroundings, however. They came from a grateful heart and were offered between other declarations of appreciation and delight, mainly about the picnic he was sharing.

"Your mum makes the best millionaire's shortbread," was one.

"This wicker hamper just makes the picnic," another.

And the ultimate accolade was, "Your mum is the Picnic Queen!"

"I helped her, don't forget!" was the immediate response of the young lady with the long red hair, sitting beside him on the tartan rug, another of her mum's thought-of-everything provisions and a reminder of where they had first met. There was a twinkle in her eye and playful mischief in her voice as she defended her sandwich-making skill.

As far as Paul was concerned life couldn't be better. This was great. Perfect.

The young pair were sitting on the grass overlooking the shore at Brown's Bay, Islandmagee, County Antrim. It was mid-July 1997, and the sun was shining from a cloudless sky. There was plenty going on around, enough to merit occasional comment, but not enough to distract attention from the pleasure of the shared picnic.

The crowning glory of the day for him was to be with the young woman whose company he so much enjoyed. She was Alison Mc Donald, a vivacious redhead. Ali, as nearly everyone called her, had been there many times before with the family but this was her first time with Paul, her best friend over the previous four years. Their friendship had deepened over the past few months particularly, and they were now 'courting,' as Paul's granny described it.

July was a free month, an in-between month, for both of them. Paul and Ali had each graduated with B.Sc. degrees in Biology with Environmental Science from Aberdeen University about six weeks earlier. Paul was due to commence training at the Police College, Tulliallen, Kincardineshire, Scotland, in early August and Alison was still unsure what plan God had for her.

That was all in the future, though, and today was today. And today was special.

Not wanting to dwell too much on the challenges of the transition from student life to full-time employment the happy day-trippers laughed and joked a lot as they recalled their experiences of University life.

On trying to determine their actual moment of initial contact Paul decided that it was in the queue for the bus to the Baptist Church on their first Sunday in Aberdeen. They were enrolled to follow the same degree course and Paul had seen Ali with dozens of others milling around at registration. It was only when they were standing beside one another in the queue to go to church that he realised they might have more in common than a study programme.

Bridge of Don Baptist Church had advertised their 'free bus to church every Sunday' widely in the student halls and he, as a Christian, had decided to take them up on their offer. Could this girl be a Christian too? On opening a conversation with her Paul discovered that she possessed what would be to him two most appealing and distinctive personal qualities. A Christian faith and a Northern Ireland accent!

Pleased to meet someone else 'from home' they had a friendly getting-to-know-you chat on the bus. Although Paul came from Bangor, Co. Down, and Ali from Greenisland, Co. Antrim, they recognised instinctively that when one is 'across the water,' anyone from Northern Ireland is somehow a kind of remote relation. They had already discovered that there were a few other 'freshers' who spoke with Ulster accents and they all sat together in church, trying to understand the rich Scottish burr.

That was the start of a growing friendship. Ali and Paul attended many of the same lectures, depending on their study modules. They shared the same spiritual interests and this led in turn to their having a similar outlook on lots of other issues. As they came to know one another better over their years at University they realised that there were a few things on which they differed, however.

One was their taste in music, the other their approach to study.

A little dog, which had strayed off on an exploratory trip from a neighbouring group had stopped for a sniff across at their promising-looking picnic basket. It was startled into a sudden sharp bark when Paul's humming of a song prompted a typical response from Ali.

"Paul, I know you like boy-bands, but please don't hum their songs in public!" she exclaimed "It's embarrassing!" When he had stopped laughing at Ali's brutal honesty Paul countered with, "Well at least its happy music! Not like all that depressing Bob Dylan stuff!" Paul was secretly quite impressed by her musical taste, but loved the banter between them. Pausing just long enough to catch Ali's smile and nod, but not long enough to allow for any response, Paul went on, "We do at least like some of the same music. Do you remember when we used to go to the Mudd Club on Monday nights? You danced and shook with your long hair flying all over the place, wearing your purple DM boots and denim jacket. Those were great nights!"

The subject of late nights provided Paul with a natural opening to introduce the second way in which he had figured they were different. "And what I could never get over about you, Ali, was that you could be up half the night and didn't worry if you couldn't concentrate on the riveting lecture on soil toxicology the next day," he continued. "You never seemed to stress out nearly as much as me. Just took everything in your stride. I remember sitting in the study room of the Soil Science building working away in my little booth, panicking at how much I still had to revise. And all that time you were lounging around on the flat roof outside in the warmth of the afternoon sun, waiting for me to take a break so we could open the biscuits!"

By this time Ali had started packing all the picnic bits and pieces back into the hamper. "Amazing how we both ended up with the same results!" she laughed, no doubt recalling how often they had joked about their study patterns over the past four years.

"I'm so glad we did now," Paul assured her. Then, changing the subject completely he said, "Let's leave this stuff in the car, and go for a walk along the beach before it is time to head home."

It was a good idea, and after crossing the road to the car park and back they negotiated a winding course round families still sitting on the grass, and on down to the beach. They walked out to the edge of the sea and strolled along, dancing out of the way of the incoming tide every now and again. At one point Paul tried to impress his friend with his skill at skimming stones across the water. It seemed that for every one that made at least three tiny splashes as it bounced across the surface four disappeared with a watery-sounding plonk, never to be seen again.

The waves were either too rough or the stones the wrong shape. Much to Ali's amusement failure was never Paul's fault!

The stone-skimming exercise was interrupted when a passenger ferry sailed out of Larne Harbour on its way across to Scotland. They stopped and watched it go, then jumped back as the wash rumbled the stones on its dash up the shore. "You would really need to stop throwing for a minute or two Paul," Ali said breathlessly, yet pretending to sound ever so serious. "You might hit somebody on that boat!"

When they came to a freshwater stream that runs out to sea at the far end of the beach Paul jokingly offered to be the gentleman and carry Ali across but she decided she would 'never hear the end of it' and suggested they go back. So they turned and retraced their steps along the water's edge, chatting and avoiding children running in and out of the sea and the watchful parents hovering around.

It was now time, they agreed, to make at least the first stage of the homeward journey. On the way back to Alison's house in the silver Metro Paul had inherited from his mum, they talked animatedly. And incessantly. Subjects touched upon ranged widely, covering topics as diverse as favourite lecturers, job prospects, branches of both family trees, buying cars and how they could possibly be sure of the will of God for their lives.

Back in the Mc Donald family home they unpacked the contents of the picnic hamper on to the kitchen table. Paul liked the space and homeliness of that kitchen. The Aga cooker, with its constant heat and kettle which always seemed to be near, or on, the boil, was an intriguing novelty for him. It was never much use to him, though, for Ali's mum Beth was constantly teasing him about not drinking either tea or coffee.

Beth chatted to them about their outing as they shared in clearing up. It wasn't long until she decided it was 'time for something to eat' and there was more cordial conversation round the scrubbed table. Paul could hardly take his eyes off Ali. He could watch her, listen to her and enjoy her genial company for ever, he felt.

It was one of those relaxed, carefree times he was loath to leave. But he had to, eventually.

Before setting off to return to Bangor later in the evening Paul arranged for Ali to come to the County Down town and meet his parents. They had met before, casually, in recent years but this was more serious now.

The drive home was performed on autopilot. Paul was making the right moves in the car and the right turns on the road but his mind wasn't on it. He was meditating on matters of the heart.

It had been a beautiful day, weather-wise.

And it had been a wonderful day, otherwise.

Paul had made a thrilling discovery and he knew Ali had made it too.

By the sea that day they had both realised something that was to mark the beginning of an amazing journey.

They were in love!

CHAPTER 2

PASSING OUT, SETTLING IN, MOVING ON.

That love was soon to encounter its first real test.

Paul and Ali had been friends for four years at University and had seen each other most days in term-time over that period. They had begun to assume that each would always be there for the other. They had talked together, studied Environmental Science together, worshipped God together and discussed the future together, often light-heartedly.

Now 'the future' had caught up with them.

On 13th August they were to be separated. That was the day Paul was due to commence his training in the Scottish Police College. Ali was remaining behind in Northern Ireland to try and find employment.

The parting was difficult.

Paul felt that an essential element of life for him was being left behind.

Ali felt that an essential element of life for her was about to disappear over the horizon.

They made the best of it, though. There were hundreds of phone calls and the occasional much-anticipated weekend when Paul drove down to Stranraer, picked Ali up from the ferry and brought her back to Edinburgh. The 14 weeks of training passed quicker than they had imagined it would, and in November Ali travelled over with Paul's parents and older brother Peter, to his passing out parade.

This was a memorable experience for all five of them.

For Paul as he had successfully completed his course and was like," Ali remarked to Paul, as they stood with some of the others, cooling off below the water of one of the falls and gazing out at the beauty of God's creation.

"It is beautiful," Paul agreed, thinking to himself how grateful he was to God for not only allowing him this glimpse into Eden, but also for the beautiful girl He had granted him the privilege of sharing it with.

Looking back on their visit to Twin Falls on the return trip to Darwin Paul and Ali each agreed it had been a naturally marvellous and spiritually exhilarating experience for both of them. Then it was back on to the road again for more Oz Experience.

Their next major stop was at Ayers Rock in the heart of the Australian Desert. Paul was anxious to climb this massive rocky outcrop in the middle of a barren plain, and Ali was equally anxious to avoid climbing it. All that exertion in the baking heat didn't appeal to her. So they reached a compromise. He climbed up it and she walked round it!

From central Australia they travelled south to Adelaide and then on to Melbourne where they both found temporary employment once more. This was essential, not because Paul and Ali particularly wanted to work, but they did need the money it would generate as funds were running low. When they reckoned they had enough saved to see them through a few more stages of their carefully planned itinerary they were away again. This time it was to New Zealand.

They arrived in Auckland on 25 October, 2000, and spent two weeks exploring the North Island. It was a time of mixed fortunes. The whales opted not to show for the six days they had attempted to go whale-watching, and they found the sulphur-scented mud of the hot springs at Rotorua fascinating, if not slightly overpowering.

Ali had been very diligent in planning their programme so that they would be with some of her relatives on the South Island for Christmas. Paul and she spent some time on the journey south, arriving with Ian and Patricia and their son Stewart, who was around the same age as the globetrotting guests, in Dunedin, or 'Edinburgh of the southern hemisphere' as it is called, on 30 November. It was great to meet up with relatives again after being 'on the road' and having no contact with their families back in Northern Ireland except the occasional phone call or letter. They had so much to talk about!

After a few enjoyable, getting-to-know-you kind of days Paul and Ali went travelling again for a short period before joining Ian, Patricia and Stewart once more, nearer Christmas. They met up at the couple's holiday home, which they called 'The Crib', in Bannock-burn, near Queenstown, to celebrate the Saviour's birth together.

It was strange to wake up on Christmas morning to find it bright, sunny and warm. What was familiar, though, was the pattern of the day. All five of them attended the special Christmas service in the morning and then it was back to the house for a lovely turkey dinner.

This was the first Christmas that Paul and Ali were to spend together and that, for each of them, was special. It was also, the first time they had been missing the festivities in their own family homes, and that was not just quite so special. The warmth of the welcome they had been afforded, and the friendship they were being shown by their 'New Zealand family' went a long way to easing the heartstrings longing for home, however.

With a thirteen hour time difference, when Boxing Day was dawning in New Zealand Christmas Day was drawing to a close in Northern Ireland, and Paul and Ali were able to use this fact to make the holiday period memorable for all. They went out to a phone box at ten in the morning on Boxing Day, used their International Calling Cards and rang home.

'Happy Christmas,' the words used frequently in the animated conversations that ensued, when nearly everyone present in the homes in Greenisland and Bangor took it in turns to speak to Paul and Ali, had now become a reality for all.

When the relatives returned to work after the holiday period it was time for the intrepid travellers to move on once more. They returned to Auckland, visiting different places of interest on the way and flew on to Fiji in mid-January. They spent a week there, relaxing and exploring Beachcomber Island before continuing to their final destination, USA.

After arriving in Los Angeles, Paul and Ali purchased Amtrak passes allowing them to travel at will on the extensive US railway network. They determined to make full use of these, visiting San Diego and the Grand Canyon before selecting destinations that had them zigzagging across the vast continent.

One of their final stop-offs in America, indeed, of their world tour was New Orleans in 'the deep south.' It was Mardi Gras time and the spring festival was in full swing. Paul and Ali had booked to stay at the edge of the French Quarter, right at the heart of the action.

There were noisy, colourful parades each day, with bands, and participants in an assortment of weird and wonderful costumes either sitting up on garish floats or singing and dancing along beside them. As the procession passed slowly along, the float attendants threw flowers and strings of brightly coloured beads into the watching crowds Paul and Ali seemed to know instinctively the right place to stand for each time they watched a parade they ended up showered with a variety of gaudy garlands and junky jewellery.

Watching the Mardi Gras parades was the focus of the day at that time, but behind the glitter and gaiety Paul and Ali were living on the edge of harsh reality. Neither of them had worked since Melbourne and resources were running low. Restaurant meals had become the exception, rather than the rule. Their eating patterns were dictated by less expensive options.

It was while having that kind of an evening meal, a sandwich from Subway, when seated on a levee gazing out across the vast expanse of the Mississippi River that Paul and Ali shared their thoughts about New Orleans. Each expressed the opinion that there was something they found mildly, but inexplicably, disconcerting, about the city and particularly its cultural festival.

Beneath all the noise and colourful clamour they felt there was an underlying sense of the occult, of voodoo, of witchcraft. It was a feeling that didn't lie comfortably with their Christian conviction. There was an odd aura of anti-God.

It was slightly scary. Weird. Awesome.

This wasn't the awesome of a marvellous feat of engineering like Sydney Harbour Bridge, the awesome of a majestic marvel of God's creation, like Twin Falls, or the awesome of celebrating Christmas in a home-from-home half-a-world away from real home. This wasn't awesome good. This was awesome evil.

Leaving New Orleans behind a few days later, Paul and Ali used their Amtrak passes to travel up the east coast of the United States to Washington and then New York. They visited the sights of 'The Big Apple' before boarding a plane bound for London and onward flight home to Belfast.

The young pair both admitted they were glad to be going home. It had been a memorable adventure and so there was much to discuss, and much to reflect upon, on the final leg of their trip. They had seen a lot, and learnt a lot about God, His world and each other. And their considerations led them to a number of conclusions.

Of all the hundreds of places they had visited they agreed that their own little country, Northern Ireland, was as beautiful, and had as much to offer, as any of them. It was definitely where they would be happy to spend the rest of their lives.

More significantly, they reckoned their happiness would only be complete if they were to spend the rest of their lives together. Thus they were resolved to 'get engaged to be married' soon after they arrived back.

Paul and Ali were both thrilled at the prospect. It was wonderful.

They had some awesome experiences over the previous twelve months. The prospect of sharing life together for months and years ahead, however, was even more awesome.

And it was the awesome of the good, the exciting, the breathtaking, variety!

CHAPTER 4
PLEASE WILL YOU MARRY ME?

The parting had been difficult when Paul first left to go to the Police College in Scotland. Going back to work in the Scottish capital and leaving Ali behind in Northern Ireland was ten times worse! They had been a year together, sharing the highs and lows of a round the world adventure.

Returning to report for duty was a lonely anticlimax for Paul, and starting to search for suitable employment in Northern Ireland was a sudden return to reality for Ali. To solve the separation situation and to advance their plans for a future in their home province, Paul applied to join the newly-created Police Service of Northern Ireland, and Ali was interviewed for, and subsequently appointed to, a position with a large accountancy firm.

They were on the phone every evening, and often during the day as well, when time and schedules permitted. It was agony being apart and they had exciting plans to discuss. Ali had always stressed, after they had decided to become engaged, that she wanted to choose her own ring. She had told Paul on more than one occasion, "I know you would like to surprise me with a ring, but don't. It's not that I wouldn't be happy with your choice or anything like that, but it's such an important and personal thing, I would just love to pick my own!"

That was fine with Paul and on Saturday 14 April 2001 they set out to let her do just that. Ali had come across to spend the weekend in Edinburgh and as they mingled with the crowds thronging Princes Street that sunny afternoon she was careful to steer her fiancé-to-be past all of what she reckoned to be the 'cheaper' jewellers. She knew exactly where she was going! It was Laing's Jewellers on Frederick Street.

When in there an understanding assistant produced a variety of rings, in different styles and a wide range of prices. They took their time over the choice. Ali had been planning for weeks for this event and she wasn't going to rush it now.

After some deliberation the ring that was Ali's outright favourite, consisting of a single diamond set in platinum, was selected and bought. What Ali didn't realise at the time was that this purchase was to the detriment of Paul's council tax, in the small flat he shared with some others, for the next couple of months. He would have to save hard to catch up, but he didn't mind.

Ali was worth every penny of it!

With Ali now obviously glowing with pride and satisfaction, the jeweller, with an eye to cashing in on the generosity he had hoped the moment would engender, turned his attention to her. "And what about something special for your fiancé to mark your engagement?" he ventured. "A nice watch perhaps?"

He followed up his introductory spiel by pointing to a number of expensive-looking samples of his wares in a glass display cabinet beside the counter. Ali stepped across, took one look at the prices and made up her mind in a second.

"No, thank you," she replied. "Not today. I'm afraid the watch Paul has is going to have to do him for a while yet!"

With that they left the jewellers 'on cloud nine.' As they rounded the corner back on to Edinburgh's most famous street once more Paul remembered something. "You know Ali, I have never formally asked you to marry me. I'll have to do that sometime!"

Ali hadn't noticed that. She had assumed all along from their conversation in the plane on the way back from America that they were just going to get married and that was it. The lack of a formal proposal hadn't caused her any sleepless nights. Playing along with the situation, however, she said, "Yes, I think you'd better."

Then stopping on the pavement and looking round for a few moments she added, "But not here!"

"Why do you say, not here?" Paul wanted to know.

"Just look where we have stopped!" the bubbling Ali laughed. "I can't go through the rest of my life telling everybody that Paul proposed to me outside Burger King. We will have to think of somewhere more exciting than here!"

The ideal location wasn't difficult to find. It was towering above them. Edinburgh Castle dominated the skyline and they decided instantly it would be a great place for such a special occasion and so they set off walking to it.

Others were trudging and puffing up the Mound and on to the top end of The Royal Mile. Not so Paul and Ali. Their hearts were happy and their feet light, and they made effortless progress. There was just one niggling concern at the back of Paul's mind, however. Had he made it clear to Ali that he meant to propose on the Castle Esplanade? He just hoped she wasn't expecting him to pay them both in, to go up on to the ramparts, or find some other location she would consider suitably romantic. His finances had already sustained a serious depletion and the admission fee to the Castle would mean saying Goodbye to another meal or two out for the both of them!

The Esplanade was lined with tour coaches and bustling with sightseers from all over the world. None of that worried Paul. He was just anxious to get the proposal under way before the possibility of entry to the Castle was even mooted. When he came to a clear space he stopped and bending down on one knee held Ali's hand, looked up into her face and asked, "Please, Ali, will you marry me?"

Both of them knew what the answer would be and they both started to cry.

Wrapped in a world of romantic reverie, the young couple were only vaguely aware that they had become the centre of attention for a group of Japanese visitors, waiting to board their coach. It was only when cameras began to click followed by a spontaneous round of applause as Paul rose to hug his bride-to-be that they realised the tourist attraction they had suddenly become!

They waved to their delighted audience as they walked back

down towards the Royal Mile and on to Paul's flat. It was time to announce their engagement to family and friends!

The first people they encountered that they knew were two of the girls who lived in the same flat as Paul. They came in and found the newly-engaged couple together in the living-room and Ali was in tears.

They were somewhat hesitant to enquire what was happening at first but then one of them ventured to ask, "Are you two having a fight? Are you splitting up or something?"

"No! No! Look!" Ali exclaimed, holding up a diamond-ring-bedecked finger. "We have just got engaged!" This announcement was followed by an ecstatic round of hugs and tears.

Paul and Ali broke free of that to inform their parents, both sets of whom had gone off to spend the weekend in Clar Ellagh Christian Endeavour Guest House in the Republic of Ireland. Paul began the process by phoning Ali's dad on his mobile and enquiring, "May I marry your daughter, please?"

"Yes, of course you can," Mr. Mc Donald told him, without the slightest hesitation.

"That's good for we just got engaged about four hours ago!" Paul replied, He had been confident of the response he would receive from his future father-in-law, and his conviction was confirmed when he heard the pop of a cork in the background.

Ali's mum had been privy to the fact that Paul and Ali were planning to become engaged that particular weekend and had come prepared to throw a mini-party for both sets of proud parents. She had brought a bottle of champagne and four plastic cups along, hidden in her luggage!

Next item on the agenda was to see if Paul could be posted back to Northern Ireland.

And mean time they could start planning a wedding!

CHAPTER 5
PLEASE DON'T MAKE ME CRY ANY MORE!

The plan was that Ali would spend the summer at home in Northern Ireland helping her mum organise the wedding. This idea suffered somewhat of a setback, however, when her new employers sent her to London to conduct a pension review.

This was great for Paul, since he and his fiancée were then on the same side of the Irish Sea, and he made frequent rail trips between the capitals. Each weekend found the couple exploring a different tourist attraction. This freedom to enjoy leisure in London stirred the travel bug within them once more, but it was different from their round-the-world adventure. They were not now on a restricted budget, considering what, when, or even if they could afford to, visit an attraction or eat a meal. They now had money to spend!

The predominant subject of conversation on these relaxed outings was the wedding later in the year and the prospect of Paul being back at work in Northern Ireland by then.

Ali's absence 'on the ground' in Greenisland meant that Beth, her mum, had to handle all the wedding arrangements. Not that she minded. Visits to possible wedding reception venues and discussions with florists and photographers kept her busy, and in constant contact with her daughter. There was one thing, though, she could not do alone and that was choose the wedding dress. A friend had agreed to make it for them, and a few visits to her by Ali on increasingly frequent trips back home as the year progressed, saw this important item begin to take shape. These tiring weekend trips were no longer necessary and planning for 'the big day' became a lot easier when Ali was recalled to Belfast to work in October.

While Ali and her mum were busily engaged discussing, then finalising wedding preparations, Paul was constantly pursuing his goal of returning to his native province. This involved sitting a series of exams with a view to becoming a member of the Police Service of Northern Ireland. These were closely followed by a fitness test and a number of interviews. Yet nothing happened.

With the summer over, autumn upon them, winter approaching and the wedding date set for 27 December 2001, Paul began to become anxious. He still didn't have an offer of a job.

At the beginning of November, unable to wait any longer for news, he contacted the recruitment branch of the PSNI and was informed his application had been successful. After all the waiting he was given a starting date of 9 December. Suddenly, from nothing happening, everything seemed to happen at once. Paul had just time to give the statutory 28 days notice to Lothian and Borders Police and make arrangements to get all his stuff home. His brother Peter came over to help with the transfer to Belfast and on Monday 9 December he began a course at the Police College in Garnerville in the city.

Ali was delighted to have her husband-to-be back on her side of the water but unfortunately their contact had to be confined to phone calls in the evening during the week, as the first four weeks of Paul's two-month training course were residential. He had to 'live in!' This meant that they were unable to see each other except at weekends, and the only weekend they had before Paul came off on Christmas leave was spent on activities that were totally alien to him, like picking menus and trying on suits!

As Christmas approached the Mc Donald family had to cope with grief in the midst of joy when Ali's maternal grandmother passed away on 23 December. This meant that with the preparations for her daughter's wedding having reached an advanced stage, Beth had to switch her attention to joining other family members in preparing for their mother's funeral. The inital thought had been to postpone the wedding but this was not considered practical, with so many arrangements having been made, so an accommodation was reached. The wedding would go ahead as planned on the 27 th, with the funeral the following day.

The marriage ceremony in Malone House, Belfast, was conducted by Dr. Joe Fell from Londonderry, with Paul's grandfather who was 93 doing a reading. Dr. Fell seemed a natural choice to preside at Ali's wedding as his family and the Mc Donalds had known each other for many years. They had developed a lifelong friendship as they had spent numerous summer holidays caravanning together.

Dr. Fell created a light moment in the service when he paused before asking Ali to pledge obedience as part of her vows. It was clear that he had seen Ali as a pleasantly single-minded girl and independent teenager as she was growing up and thus invited her to 'love, honour, and...' There was a wry smile and a momentary delay before going to on committing her to 'obey!'

When the service was over the group of guests moved into an adjoining room for the reception. It was all so relaxed with no journey to be made between different venues allowing them to catch up with all the latest news of family and friends.

After the meal Ali's dad and Paul's brother both spoke. It was no surprise to Paul that Lawson Mc Donald had so much to say about how great a young woman Ali was, and what a treasure her new husband had found. What did surprise him, though, was the positive nature of Peter's speech. He had half expected some amusing, and possibly embarrassing recollections of childhood and some good-natured ribbing, but it wasn't like that. The main theme of his speech was about how he too loved Ali, and how his young brother and she seemed such a perfect match!

Ali had found this all touching to the point of being overwhelming.

As the groom rose to speak she looked up at him imploringly before he had the chance to say anything. Her eyes were swimming with tears, and they carried a message that came across more distinctly than words could ever express.

It was simply, 'Please don't make me cry anymore!'

Paul tried to respond to her unspoken but unmistakeable plea by keeping his speech lighter, focusing on how he and 'the now Mrs.

Watson' felt God had brought them together, on some of the interesting experiences of their University and world-tour days, and their plans for the future, as far as they could possibly see.

When the reception finished the celebrations didn't. They just switched venue. Ali's parents invited all who were free to join Paul and Ali and both families at 'open house' at their home in Station Road, Greenisland.

It was late when the newly-weds left there to set off on their honeymoon. When well-wishers asked Paul if the honeymoon destination was a secret he normally replied cheerily, "No, not at all! We have booked an apartment in Costa-del-Carrick!"

What he really meant was they were going to spend the first months of their married lives in a flat Ali's dad owned in Carrickfergus! And it was only two miles down the road from the Mc Donald family home.

The location was of little consequence to Paul and Ali. They had worked in Sydney and relaxed in Fiji. They had watched the sun rise over the Great Barrier Reef and set over New Orleans. They had marvelled at the skill of men in the bustle of high-rise Hong Kong and the wonderful creation of God in the Australian outback.

There had been many special moments during their round the world tour. They had only been close friends then, though.

As they stood that night, arms round each other and a glass of champagne in the free hand, gazing out at the lights reflected on Belfast Lough, this was infinitely more special! They were now husband and wife.

There could be no lie-in on their first full day as Mr. and Mrs. Watson, however. It was up early to begin the drive to Warrenpoint, Co. Down for grandma's funeral. On returning to 'Costa-del-Carrick' that evening Paul and Ali felt they were now really on honeymoon, but it was to be short. They enjoyed a few blissful days together and then they were separated once more.

Paul had to return to his training course in Garnerville on Wednesday 3 January, 2002. And he had to live in for another fortnight!

CHAPTER 6

COULD THIS BE IT?

The two weeks of separation soon passed and Paul and Ali settled down to appreciate the joys of establishing a pattern of married life. Ali was working in Belfast and as Paul's course in Garnerville was scheduled to continue until July they were able to spend every evening and weekend together. This was a delight they took for granted at the time, but began to look back on fondly, later in the year, when Paul began working duty shifts with the PSNI.

During the months of their engagement they had determined that one of their priorities when married and living in Northern Ireland would be to find a suitable church to attend. As committed Christians, worshipping and serving God, both individually and as a couple, was a primary issue in their lives. They were anxious to find a church with an active and acceptable spiritual vision and where they could be part of a caring community of believers, somewhere in the locality.

Among the first places of worship they decided to try was Glenabbey church. Ali recalled having been there a number of years before with a friend, and enjoying it. When she contacted this friend Ali was told they would be made very welcome. She also advised that 'Glenabbey', as it had come to be known, had moved to larger premises on the Ballycraigy Road in Newtownabbey, to accommodate a steadily growing membership.

Accepting the news of growth as an encouraging sign, Paul and Ali set out to find this place of worship in its new location one Sunday morning. Their quest did not turn out just as straightforward as they had expected it to be, however. The problem, as they were later to discover, was that they were searching for a building meeting their conditioned concept of what 'a church' should look like. And they couldn't find one!

Up and down the road they drove, from where they turned in, right out to cows in fields, without success, until Ali spotted a little notice on a wall. It was at the end of what appeared to be the access road to a housing development. Realising that they were fast running out of time and options they followed the road down between the houses for a short distance until they came upon a large gravel area which seemed to be serving as a car park for something. They drove in, adding their car to the large number of vehicles clustered in a kind of find-a-space-if-you-can-get-it order around what appeared to be a huge warehouse.

Paul switched off the engine and spoke, to ask himself as much as Ali, "Can this be it?"

They sat for a moment, considering, but when two of the cars which had followed them in stopped, and their occupants stepped out, Paul and Ali felt they had their answer. It was Ali who voiced what her husband had also noticed. "I think it must be," she concluded. "I see a couple of those young guys who got out of that last car, and are now heading over to what must be the door, are carrying Bibles."

That was as sure a sign as they could wish for that 'this was it' and so they joined the others strolling from the edges of the car park to converge on the door. The friend whom Ali had contacted was waiting for them, with another young lady, and they all walked into 'the warehouse' together.

This was different from most churches Paul and Ali had ever been to before. Different, but positively different. There were no stained glass windows and no formal pews. There was instead a heart-warming, welcoming, worshipping atmosphere. Everything appeared so alive. There seemed to be a buzz of spiritual anticipation, an expectation that something worth waiting for was about to take place.

As the service began, then progressed, Paul and Ali felt increasingly at ease as each new phase unfolded. The music was lively and the pieces led by the 'worship team' were played and sung with a remarkable combination of enthusiasm and reverence which appealed to both of them. Later in the service they found the Bible study session conducted by Gilbert Lennox, the teaching elder, both practical and challenging.

That first morning at Glenabbey made a very favourable impression on the newly-weds and so they continued to attend for another few weeks before facing up to the question Ali posed, one Sunday morning on the way there. It was, "Do you think we should stick with Glenabbey, Paul, or should we take our time and visit a few more churches before committing ourselves?"

"I don't really think we need to see other places," was Paul's considered reply. "Glenabbey ticks all the boxes as far as we are concerned. Why try anywhere else?"

That was how Ali felt too and so they began to become more involved in the range of Christian activities their chosen church had to offer. They were soon to find the 20's – 30's home group in particular of great spiritual benefit. That was where, when they started to attend, they not only met a number of friendly individuals and couples in their own age group but also came to appreciate practically the encompassing support of belonging to a huge, caring Christian family.

Having found themselves a permanent spiritual home Paul and Ali then concentrated their attention on purchasing a new physical home, namely a house of their own to accommodate the family they hoped to have in days to come. Ali's dad, in whose flat they had been living contentedly, kept popping in now and again with property brochures. He knew the criteria for the house Paul and Ali wanted. In addition to the usual requirements of being structurally sound and in a quiet area it should also be within striking distance of Glenabbey and it would be good too if it could be near Ali's parent's home in Greenisland. The young wife had designs on becoming a young mother, and having her mum 'on hand' could prove a decided plus factor should that ever come to pass.

Many brochures and a few house-viewings later Paul and Ali found the place they had been looking for. A four-bedroom house in Greenisland met all their predetermined requirements and after the agreements were signed they moved into their new home in August 2002. They worked on the property during the autumn, buying suitable furniture and adding a number of personal touches to the decor. The young married couple shared a plan to transform the house they had bought into a loving family home.

They hadn't long to wait to fulfil the next phase of that dream either for in the spring of 2003 Ali was thrilled to discover she was expecting their first child. During the summer that followed Paul and she attended ante-natal classes where they met other parents to be, some of whom were, like themselves, embarking on the experience of parenthood for the first time. As the pregnancy advanced Paul and Ali thanked God for the promise of a baby and prayed for a successful birth and wisdom in the raising of him or her. With the enthusiasm Beth, who adored children, showed for the coming grandchild, Ali recognised the divine help they had requested would no doubt be augmented by some loving maternal advice.

The new family member was due to arrive in the autumn and on Thursday 9 October Ali had gone out to the ladies' cell-group of their Glenabbey home-group as usual. When she returned home later, though, she knew the time was fast approaching when they would have to make an important move. They waited around at home for a few more hours, 'just to be sure,' then Ali made the decision.

"I think it's time we made it down to the Hospital," she concluded.

Waiting-to-be fathers don't usually need to be told that twice, and Paul was no exception. He and Ali were at the door of Belfast's Royal Maternity Hospital in a very short time despite having to make a frantic return home after being only ten minutes out on their journey. This was to pick up Ali's medical notes which Paul was supposed to bring, but had left behind on the kitchen table in all the rush!

What a thrill it was for them when their first child, a son whom they had decided to call Mark, was born at 7.15 on the morning of Friday 10 October. It was wonderful. The new parents gazed in awe at tiny hands and feet, a wisp of dark hair and a perfectly proportioned face - eyes, nose and mouth. And what they found so exciting to appreciate, he was their son!

They came down to earth with a bump when a nurse enquired if they had any nappies with them, and they had to confess they hadn't. Ali had bought them as part of her preparations weeks before, but with other matters on their minds the previous night they had forgotten to bring them in.

All the excited phone calls giving delighted family members birth details of their new baby had been made when Paul had to get back on the mobile once more. He had to make an emergency call to his mother-in-law. "When you are coming down here later, Beth, could you please bring a few packets of disposable nappies with you?" was his request.

Beth didn't mind this at all! It gave her good reason to make an immediate trip to the hospital to see her daughter, now a mother herself, and catch her first glimpse of baby Mark. When visiting time came others arrived to congratulate the young parents of their 'lovely little boy' but when it was over Paul remained. It would be important to allow Ali to have a sleep if possible so he promised to stay quiet for a while. What he really did was watch the opening match of the rugby World Cup, with Australia playing Argentina, on the bedside TV. The proud dad was cradling his four-hour old son in his arms, and looking down at the sleeping infant at one stage told him, "You are never too young to watch rugby!"

Although ecstatic about their little son in hospital, euphoria was replaced by reality when the Watson family became three instead of two in their Greenisland home. Baby Mark wasn't a very good sleeper and didn't seem to have learnt that human beings were programmed by nature to sleep at night. Any little sleeping he chose to do was mostly during the day!

That was when Ali was so thankful they had bought a house

close to that of her parents. Beth was a tremendous help to her daughter, who referred to her mum as 'my rock.' She shopped for anything the Watson trio needed and brought round plated dinners to save Ali having to cook. Then when Paul returned to work she came over to care for Mark so her daughter could have an hour or two's rest in preparation for what was usually a restless night ahead.

Friends kept assuring Paul and Ali that this phase would soon pass and Mark would 'settle into a routine.' They often found this hard to believe when trying to pacify a thoroughly 'unsettled' baby at four o'clock in the morning.

Their friends were right, though. Mark did become easier to work with as the weeks passed and his parents became more confident in managing him. Paul and Ali could now begin to enjoy their baby son, watching his every stage of development with interest. Both sets of parents and their friends from the Glenabbey house group were a constant support and when Peter and his wife Niky had their first child, Paddy, early in 2004 Mark had a boy cousin and Ali found it reassuring to have someone around her own age in the family circle with whom to share 'baby stories.'

Ali had left work before Mark was born, declaring she wanted to be a full time mother to her child and this left her free to bring up her growing son and enjoy regular rendezvous with Niky and Paddy. During the summer of 2004 Peter and Paul spent some of their days off joining their wives and sons on occasional days out to places of interest as far apart as Tollymore Forest Park in Co. Down and The Giant's Causeway in North Antrim. On these outings the pair of brothers talked about work and sport. Their wives, the two young mothers, by contrast, became engrossed in comparing notes on baby-centred topics such as feeding preferences or sleeping patterns.

This close family friendship with Peter and Nicky continued as Mark and Paddy left off being intriguing babies and advanced into becoming inquisitive toddlers. Every phase of this progress was reported to grandparents and family friends by the proud parents.

In 2005 Ali told Niky that she was pregnant again with a second baby expected in August of that year. Paul and she were delighted that Mark was to have a little brother or sister. It represented a further step towards their vision of a happy home echoing to the sound of happy children. In the middle of the year Niky got back to Ali with her news. She was expecting again too, just three months later, in November!

The joy of parenthood returned for Ali and Paul when Euan was born on 16 August. They were 'over the moon' to have a second son. Mark was very inquisitive about this little brother he now had. As baby Euan grew Mark began to show his love by giving him lots of kisses and tickling his tummy. This was evidence of a loving bond that both parents were thrilled to watch develop in the ensuing months.

Life was easier as parents, second time round, their friends were equally supportive and Peter and Nicky added to the happy mix by having a daughter, Aoife, in November as anticipated. Now the complete baby discussion scenario was set to advance to stage two. At this level it was not only the actions of the babies that came in for intense scrutiny and prolonged discussion. The reactions of the rapidly developing toddlers received frequent mention as well.

For Paul and Ali the spring of 2006 was an exciting, happy, busy time. The boys were progressing normally, Paul was busy at work, and Ali was in daily contact with her mum for advice, for babysitting or simply for a leisurely chat.

Everyone was thankful for and at ease with, the family situation in which they all felt so blessed.

Yet no one had any idea how quickly, or how dramatically, things were set to change...

CHAPTER 7
YOU OUGHT TO GET DOWN THERE QUICKLY!

That spring Ali's mum began complaining of a very sore back. At first she blamed it on perhaps twisting it when working in the garden or maybe even lifting one of the boys. Or could it be something to do with the fact she was a diabetic? Possibly a change of treatment for her diabetes would afford some relief.

When the pain continued to get worse rather than better she went to her local GP who in turn arranged appointments with a series of consultants and specialists. A battery of tests was carried out but nothing conclusive showed up at first.

At the beginning of June 2006 another sets of tests eventually revealed the source of Beth's, by then almost unbearable, pain and the gravity of the underlying condition causing it.

She had thyroid cancer.

This news came as a shattering blow to her husband and family.

Beth, who was Lawson's loving wife, Ali's 'rock' and a source of endless support with Mark and Euan, was critically ill. When she was admitted to the Cancer Centre at Belfast City Hospital a few days later the hub on which the wheel of the Mc Donald family turned was suddenly removed, throwing them all into a state of deep shock.

Ali, who relied on her mum so much found coming to terms with her sudden illness, her absence from home and her obviously deteriorating physical condition particularly difficult. It was all so unreal.

Her mind kept her in a detached, mystical, make-believe world that kept saying, 'This can't be happening to my mum... to us... to me.' When she drove into the grounds of Belfast City Hospital, parked and crossed to the Cancer Centre, however, a harsh dose of reality set in. 'You'd better get used to it,' it said. 'For it is.'

Within days of being admitted to Ward 1 of the recently-opened Cancer Centre Beth's pain became excruciating, and she wasn't responding to any treatment.

Although her discomfort continued unabated Beth maintained a radiant Christian witness in the ward. She never complained of anything except the awful pain, and relatives and medical staff alike were constantly amazed at, and indeed buoyed by, her attitude and fortitude.

Beth's younger sister Beenie, her best friend, and reason for Lawson's very large phone bills, visited her every day to sit at the bedside and help to nurse her sister. Beenie did not know all those years ago when she followed her sister into the nursing profession that she would one day have to nurse Beth. She had always been there to help Beth with whatever she needed and the two of them were able to chat, laugh and cry with one another during the many hours they were to spend together in the coming days.

Another regular visitor to Room 3, the little side-ward off the main ward, was Rev. Trevor Gribben minister of Whiteabbey Presbyterian Church. He told Lawson more than once of going in to see Beth, prepared to read appropriately encouraging and comforting Scriptures and pray with her. The hope was that his presence and prayers would somehow prove a source of inspiration or at least consolation to the patient whose condition had become more painful, even pitiful. He confessed, however, that if his visit hadn't achieved its intended purpose with Beth although he was quietly confident it had, he certainly had come away blessed by the encounter. "There is a real glow of the Holy Spirit surrounding Beth in that room," he remarked after one such visit.

With the disease not responding to any of the treatment administered Beth was soon on high doses of morphine to alleviate the pain and becoming visibly weaker by the day. She had just been in hospital a little over two weeks when Dennis, Beenie's husband, arrived at the door of Lisburn Road Police Station, where Paul was on night duty, at around 3 o'clock in the morning.

He enquired if Paul was available, and when he was located he wasn't altogether surprised to find Dennis waiting for him with disturbing news. "Beth is very low," he told him. "I think you ought to get down there as soon as you possibly can."

It was an urgent message and one he knew he couldn't ignore. When Paul had arranged cover for what he had been working on, a colleague drove him the short distance down to the City Hospital.

Beth was lying face down on the bed, as she was forced to do because of the persistent pain, when her son-in-law entered the room.

She was aware of him coming in and looked up as he approached the bed. Beth had always been glad to see Paul arrive anywhere, anytime, and invariably had a cheery greeting for him. This time was no exception, regardless of the circumstances.

"Hi Paul," she began. Then after pausing to study his appearance from head to toe, went on, "It's the first time I've seen you in uniform. And you're very handsome!"

Well aware of how his mum-in-law had never failed to appreciate a joke, Paul replied, "That's just the medication talking now!"

Paul stayed just a short time, said 'Goodbye' to someone he had long since come to cherish, was taken back up to the Station, collected his car and made for home. When he arrived at the house it was 5 o'clock in the morning and he and his terribly worried wife did a changeover. When Paul reported how ill her mum was, Ali's instinctive reaction was to want to be with her, so she left as soon as she was ready.

It was already clear on that bright summer morning, Wednesday 21 June, 2006, and Belfast was stirring into life as Ali drove into the city. She met milk vans, post vans and bread delivery lorries all preparing to carry the residents through the humdrum routine of another day.

None of that registered with her. She was in a daze of detachment. All she could think of was her mum. In pain. Probably dying.

Ali's only sister Janet and her husband Douglas had booked to fly in from Inverness, Scotland, where they lived, later that day. Janet had been in constant contact with her dad and Ali and gathered from what they reported of conversations with medical staff that her mum was now gravely ill. Her life expectancy was now being measured, not in months or even days, but hours.

With Lawson, Ali and Beenie all present at Beth's bedside Paul met his brother- and sister-in-law arriving off their flight at 2.30 pm and rushed them down the M2 motorway at top speed. They went straight to the hospital room where Beth was lying in a semi-conscious state.

Janet went straight over, kissed her mum, and then stepped back to join the others, to wait as they knew, for God to call her to Himself. And in half-an-hour it happened. It was as though she had waited for Janet to arrive in from Scotland before she left for heaven.

Beth was gone.

There were tears and hugs all round. What were the family going to do without their anchor? It was hard to imagine.

The initial shock of grief gave way over the next day or two to the consolation of recollection. As people came to see Lawson and the bereaved family at their Greenisland home, stories abounded of the selfless kindness with which Beth lived life and the spiritual courage with which she faced death.

Saturday 24 June was a memorable day, which began with a brief private service for the immediate family. This was held at the home Beth had shared for so many years so happily with Lawson and the daughters of whom she felt justly proud. Now, though, the lightness of a life of love and joy was replaced by a heavy cloud of sorrow and loss.

Shortly after the service in the home the family joined a capacity crowd packing Whiteabbey Presbyterian Church for the public Thanksgiving Service. During this service there were tears of grief and sympathy and the occasional ripple of laughter. Rev. Trevor Gribben alternated the solemnity of expressing condolences on behalf of the gathered mourners with a few amusing anecdotes recalling examples of what Beth had said to her husband, Ali and Janet on occasions during the precious years they had spent together.

Pervading the entire proceedings, however, whether the congregation were silent in sorrow or allowing themselves a momentary lapse into subdued laughter, was a tremendous sense of the presence of God. It was clear from all the tributes paid that Beth had been a Christian whose life had made an impact for God, and for good. Rev. Gribbben stressed that she was now in heaven, not because of her exemplary life, but because of her faith in Christ, of which her good works were a natural by-product. Nor was she gone forever. She had merely gone ahead.

The days of mourning prior to Beth's funeral were complicated by an important decision the family had to make. As with Paul and Ali's wedding, when a funeral had to be held back to allow it to go ahead, so Lawson and those close to him had to decide whether or not to go to a wedding following the funeral of their dearly-loved wife and mother.

Beenie's son, Alastair Alexander, was due to marry his fiancée Alison on Sunday 2 July, in King's Lynn, Norfolk, England. Beth had already accepted an invitation to attend on behalf of Lawson and herself and Paul had booked a holiday flat in which they could all stay as a family group.

The big question was, should they, could they, go?

A few phone calls and some serious discussion resolved the issue. Paul and Ali believed that 'mum' would have wanted them to go, so they did, and Lawson came too.

Despite the sense of loss felt so keenly by the husband who was now missing his director of home affairs, and Ali who had been abruptly deprived of her 24 / 7 counselling service, they all managed to enjoy, in a muted kind of way, the couple's 'big day.' Many of those present were aware of the situation and were most caring and sympathetic. The group exchanged many stories of happy times with Beth as they sat together in the sunshine watching the boys play with the new bride and groom. It served as a welcome, albeit only temporary, escape for the Mc Donald family from the heart-rending anxiety and grief of the previous few weeks

There were a succession of not so happy 'big days' appearing over the horizon, when they all got back home, though. No one was sure how he or she was going to cope without Beth. They were sailing into uncharted waters.

Ali found it devastating.

CHAPTER 8
HOW AM I GOING TO TELL MY DAD?

On their return from England, Ali had an appointment at the Family Planning Clinic on Thursday 6 July, 2006, and it was during a routine examination that the doctor discovered what he described as 'a cervical polyp.' Ali was assured that this was not unusual but that she would be referred to the Mater Hospital for further procedures.

Initially Paul and Ali thought nothing about it, but as time went on the notion of 'a polyp' triggered a sense of unease in Ali's mind. What if there was something wrong? Why were 'they' so slow in getting back to her?

When she hadn't heard anything by the end of October she rang the Mater Hospital and was told that hers had been classed as 'a non-urgent referral.' Not entirely satisfied with this Ali mentioned some worrying symptoms she was experiencing to her GP, and an appointment was arranged for 17 January 2007.

It was a crisp and sunny winter day when the young couple went up to the Mater Hospital on that date. They put their arms around each other, if not for warmth, for comfort and reassurance of each other's presence as they walked in. Paul had to leave Ali for a short time to allow the doctor to examine her but when the nurse called him in he knew instinctively something wasn't quite right. This wasn't just 'a polyp.' The nurse didn't say anything more than that the doctor wished to speak to both of them

Ali sat on the only chair in the small room as she was feeling decidedly uncomfortable from the test. The physical discomfort was but a small matter compared with the mental turmoil the last 30 minutes had given rise to, though. There was no seat for Paul, but he didn't need one. He walked the short distance from the window to the door, and back to put his arm around his wife, and then off on the extra-short circuit again. Keeping mobile allowed him some relief from the mental pressures of the moment. Conversation came only in short bursts. What was there to say? Yet, anyway.

A doctor and nurse returned with the results after what seemed like an interminable wait. Paul and Ali were in tears by then and what they were about to learn afforded them little incentive to dry their eyes. It confirmed what they had feared.

Although neither member of the medical team actually used 'the C word,' what they said would have it shooting immediately into the mind of any intelligent individual. And Paul and Ali were reasonably intelligent individuals.

"The test has shown a growth in your cervix, Ali, and a smaller secondary growth also," was the first piece of gut-wrenching information they were given. "It will most likely require radiotherapy and /or even a hysterectomy." These two hammer blows were followed, after a few moments left for them to sink in, by the proposed course of action. "We will be sending your test results across to an oncology team at the City Hospital, and they will discuss them at their multi-disciplinary team meeting next Wednesday. They will then call you for a consultation soon after that."

Next Wednesday! But this was only Thursday!

Paul and Ali were already distressed at the news they had anticipated, then been given. How were they going to face at least another six days in a quandary of questions? It was set to be a domain of doubt and dread, a state of conjecture and confusion.

The medics left the room when they had answered the few queries Paul and Ali struggled to articulate. They told the devastated couple to remain as long as they liked, and not to leave until they felt ready.

Ali sat and Paul stood. Both silent. Both in tears.

It must have taken them nearly ten minutes to compose themselves sufficiently to walk out on legs that felt weak and hollow.

They had to go through a maternity ward to reach a lift in the corridor and as they were crossing it they met one of their neighbours who was a midwife. She greeted them and Paul and Ali stumbled something in reply.

Logical thought didn't come easily to them at that moment. Coherent speech was a definite impossibility. When out of the Mater Hospital they crossed the road into a car park at the side of the former Crumlin Road Jail. The walls of the now-derelict building seemed an added menace somehow. It was as though light was closing into darkness and freedom was giving way to restriction.

When they reached the car they sat for another moment of stunned, shared silence, before Paul said, "We have to tell somebody. I'm going to ring Peter." He and Ali were close to his brother and sister-in-law, and they were aware of the appointment.

On hearing Paul's voice Peter's immediate question was, "Well, how did it go?"

"Not good," Paul replied. "The doctors think Ali has cancer." It was stark news, and came bluntly from a mind struggling to come to terms with it.

Now it was Peter's turn to be shocked. As couples with families they had shared many carefree times together. Suddenly that all seemed so far in the past. What was there to say to this, though, in the here and now? It was dreadful.

His response was a muted, considerate, "That's awful. When will you know any more?"

"We are to have an appointment over at the City Hospital sometime after next Wednesday, and we will probably hear more then," Paul told him. It was all he could say, for it was all he knew. And Peter thought, as he and Ali did, that the days before this next appointment were going to seem torturously long.

When Paul rang off he and Ali drove out towards home. In the car Ali's concern was focussed not on herself, but on others. Especially her dad. "How am I going to tell my dad, Paul?" she asked, in a turmoil of emotion.

"We will work it out," Paul assured her, though he hadn't a clue how. He appreciated how difficult it was going to be for Lawson. A double whammy. First Beth. And now possibly Ali. His wife and his daughter, both in the same year.

Ali agonised over it all the way back to the babysitter's house where they had left the boys off before going up to the Mater.

That threw up another big problem. As Mark rushed out and Euan toddled out on unsteady feet to meet their parents, Ali couldn't possibly restrain herself. She burst into a flood of tears. Taking them one by one, and at one stage both of them together, she hugged them and hugged them.

How and when would she ever be able to tell her two boys? Or would she ever need to?

Perhaps she was painting too black a picture for herself. Could next week possibly afford any hope? She wouldn't talk to many about it until after then, she determined.

She could, and would, though, talk it over with Paul, and God. Often.

CHAPTER 9

WHITE COATS AND WHEELCHAIRS

When Sunday came, Paul, Ali and the boys were out at the morning service in Glenabbey as usual. Ali knew that if there was any solace to be found in this anxious period of nearly-knowing but nonetheless somehow-desperately-hoping, it would be in collective communion with God, and close contact with Christian friends. The few who knew of Paul and Ali's position were quietly, and they assured, prayerfully, supportive. It was reassuring to have such friends and the young parents were able to gather some crumbs of comfort from the worship, the Bible teaching and the overall awareness of the Divine Presence.

It was in one sense welcome news when they received the appointment they had been expecting, but in another it merely served to confirm their worst fears. It was for Thursday, so that meant they wouldn't have to wait longer than a week to hear more. That was the only good that could be said about it. The fact it was for the Outpatients Department at the Cancer Centre in the grounds of Belfast City Hospital, could not, they knew, be considered in any way a positive sign.

Paul and Ali tried valiantly to keep life at home as normal as possible for the boys' sake, but when their sons were out or in bed, they discussed the implications of what they already thought they knew. Or they made phone calls to concerned relatives or took phone calls from concerned friends.

It was a relief, eventually, to arrive outside the Cancer Centre that Thursday morning after what seemed like one of the longest weeks of their lives. It was a relief, though, only because the waiting was now over, and at last there was going to be an end to all the apprehension and speculation.

The memories the sight of the building evoked in each of them, however, did little to set their troubled minds at ease. The last time Paul had walked out of it seven months before he had just said 'Goodbye' to his friend and mother-in-law, Beth.

She was dying, then.

The last time Ali had walked out of it she had just said 'Goodbye' to her mum who was her pillar of strength, her first port in a storm at a time like this.

She had just died.

Another thought struck Paul as they crossed from the car park to the Cancer Centre. The medical profession must consider the treatment of cancer in all its forms a top priority, he mused. They have this massive modern building dedicated exclusively to it. If Ali had it, she certainly wouldn't be the only one. There must be thousands of patients treated in a place like this.

This was interesting, and accurate, as a general observation, but downright disturbing as a personal reflection. He had the wife he loved, the mother of their children, passing in through the spacious entrance hall by his side. She was a precious person, not a cold statistic.

They hadn't been long in the waiting area until Ali was called. The doctor wanted to examine her before making any disclosure on the nature or gravity of her condition.

Paul sat outside for what seemed like forever. He was agitated to such an extent he couldn't even bring himself to read the rugby pages in the sports section of one of the spare newspapers lying around.

Paying close attention to all the comings and goings in the busy reception area served to divert his thinking from what was happening in the nearby consulting room. What a mix of people, in what a variety of circumstances and what a display of human emotion was on show in that confined space.

There were people in wheelchairs, with anxious looking relatives in attendance.

There were men and women in white coats, walking through with an obvious sense of purpose.

There were people with no hair. What surprised Paul was that it didn't seem to bother them one bit.

There were what Paul took to be young doctors, or perhaps they were students, passing him in small groups, talking seriously. Could it be about their last patient or their next exam? How young some of them looked. They must still be at University, he concluded.

There were others like himself. Relatives, or friends or maybe even neighbours doubling as drivers, all waiting for a patient to appear back beside them from somewhere. A few of the less uptight of them were passing the time by keeping in touch with the big world beyond the building, talking or texting on mobile phones.

There were nurses. A group of four of them suddenly burst into Paul's line of vision from a door at the side. They were probably off on their lunch break as they were heading round towards the ground floor coffee shop. What Paul found hard to believe was that they were laughing and joking as they walked. They appeared not to have a care in the world.

Did they not know what was happening to him? Did nobody care? He was swimming about in the depths of despair. How could people who worked in a place like this actually dare to **laugh**?

Eventually a member of the medical team came out looking for Paul, to invite him to join the others already in the consulting room. Ali was sitting on a chair at one side. She was already in tears.

Looking up at her husband as he entered she stated what he had already assumed, "It's cancer."

Instinctively, and totally regardless of the fact that there were two others present, Paul went straight across to Ali and hugged her. They both needed the comfort of each others' arms at that moment.

When Paul was ready to hear more he released Ali from the embrace and took the unoccupied chair waiting for him. There were two other ladies in the room he discovered, on becoming more conscious of his surroundings.

They had been sitting quietly and patiently as the shattered young couple struggled to come to terms with what they now had confirmed. No conjecture now. No faint hopes. No what-ifs? This was it. The two clinicians had been in this situation before and were well able to cope with it. They were in no hurry and would give Paul and Ali as long as they needed.

With Paul settled beside his distraught wife they waited until they reckoned the time was right before introducing themselves. One was an oncologist, a sympathetic lady who didn't appear to be much older than Ali herself, and the other a radiotherapy practitioner. The doctor began by outlining the proposed treatment which she explained had been discussed and decided upon the day before by a team of oncologists. It would be specifically targeted at Ali's condition.

At one point the doctor was almost apologetic. "I'm sorry she said. "But I'm afraid one of the side effects of the drugs we will be using is that it will leave you infertile, Alison."

Ali looked across at Paul, and it was he who gave their reaction to that disclosure. "Well, that will be OK," he said. "We had decided that our two boys were all the family we wanted, and now if we know they are all we can have, we will be happy at that."

"When you mention side-effects," Ali interjected before the oncologist could continue, "What about my hair? Will the drugs make me lose my hair?"

Looking across at the patient's flaming mane of red hair the doctor could understand her concern and was glad to be able to respond reassuringly, "No. I am pleased to say that the particular drug we will be using in your case does not cause hair loss."

She went on to say that although the course of treatment they were prescribing would be both intensive and tiring, the likelihood of success was good.

This positive prediction, coupled with the assurance that Ali was not going to suffer hair loss were two encouraging aspects of what was otherwise a pretty discouraging outlook, in the immediate future at least.

Ali was to have six weeks of treatment, with chemotherapy on the Mondays of the first five weeks and radiotherapy on the remaining 25 weekdays of the period. The final piece of information the young couple were anxious to know was when this programme was scheduled to begin.

"We will let you know, definitely, in a few days time," the doctor told them. "But it will be as soon as possible." Now there remained nothing left for them to do but to go home and prepare themselves for the days ahead. The time had come to inform the wider circle of family and friends, and particularly the members of their caring church fellowship, of the trauma that had entered their lives.

The news caused deep shock in, and evoked genuine sympathy from, all who heard it. Numerous letters and cards, texts and calls, were received every day. The Christian community in Glenabbey united in wholehearted prayer support for the young couple and their two little boys. They meant so much to them.

Although facing the prospect of intensive chemo- and radio-therapy Ali continued to be more concerned about others than herself. She worried constantly about her dad.

'Was it 'really fair' on him?' she wondered. Losing his wife to cancer, and then learning his daughter had it too, all inside six months. And what about their two lovely sons? Mark and Euan. She wasn't going to be able to afford them the attention they were used to from their mum when she was having treatment.

Paul and she experienced a whole range of emotions. Again. They were in another in-between waiting period. And it was hard.

Not for the first time in the past three months everything seemed surreal. It felt once more as though they were actors in a drama being played out on a different planet.

There were times, particularly when they had a card or a call, saying, 'We are praying for you,' that they cried out in prayer themselves.

Then there were other occasions, tempered more by practical than spiritual emphases, when they found themselves slipping, involuntarily, into total dispondency.

That was when they asked despairingly, "Why is God allowing this to happen to us?"

CHAPTER 10

TRYING DAYS AND PIZZA NIGHTS

The programme of treatment the oncology team had planned for Ali began in early February 2007. It was scheduled to last six weeks, and they were to prove six hard, testing weeks for Ali, her husband and family. There were, however, dotted through those days, occasional lighter moments, like shafts of sunlight sneaking through grey clouds to provide fleeting spots of brightness on a dark sea surface.

Paul was granted compassionate leave to care for the boys, so most of the transport to and from the Centre for Ali's daily radiotherapy sessions was shared by Ali's dad and aunt Beenie. It was on Monday evenings, when Ali had to remain in the Centre overnight for her chemotherapy, that Paul was able to spend more time with his wife, supporting her in every way possible. Ali's aunt Margaret looked after the boys to allow him to stay up with Ali until late in the evening as the chemotherapy was administered.

These weekly chemo sessions were not made any easier by what the family had gone through just eight months earlier. They took place in Ward 1, the ward in which Ali's mum was treated, and on arriving each Monday her daughter had to pass the side-ward in which she passed away. Ali found this difficult, particularly during the initial sessions. Recognising her unease, Paul spoke to the nursing staff, many of whom had cared for Beth also, and obtained an assurance from them that Ali would never be treated in that room.

Ali usually spent these overnight treatments in a four-bed bay in Ward 1 and Paul and she quickly came to know some of the others there for similar reasons on Monday evenings as well. At the beginning of the evening, before the chemo had abolished her appetite, Ali often felt like sampling something tasty.

So, it would seem, did at least one of the other patients.

Aware from their travels abroad and nights in at home that his wife was extremely fond of pizza, Paul brought one in with him when coming to see Ali on the second Monday evening of her chemotherapy sessions.

As soon as Paul opened the flat pizza container the appetising aroma of its contents escaped and floated around the ward. An American girl, lying in the bed opposite Ali had her almost redundant taste buds invigorated. Although she hadn't been able to eat much for some time she called over, "I would really love a pizza!"

Paul stepped across and said, "I could go out and get you one if you like, but are you sure your doctor would allow you to eat pizza?"

"I don't know whether he would or not," the girl replied. "But if you would get me one I would take responsibility for it!"

When Ali began eating hers Paul set out to purchase another one for her friend. This was the beginning of a pizza pattern. Every Monday evening Paul brought in, or went out and bought in, sufficient to share with all who felt like a piece.

This provided a welcome opener to what was set to become a deteriorating night ahead for them all. It helped to create a cheerful atmosphere in the ward. Eating helped everyone enjoy a sense of satisfaction. Chatting helped create a sense of shared situation.

If it weren't for the sets of medical equipment stationed beside each bed one would almost be tempted to conclude there wasn't a lot wrong with the women in those beds.

The equipment was there, however, for a very specific reason. The women in the beds in that bay were very ill.

This was patently evident the following morning. Ali would be typical of them all. When she was ready for home she was ready to go straight to bed. She felt drained, listless and sick. The awful weakness was wearisome, the nausea far from nice.

There were two things Ali found particularly perturbing during those days when travelling back and forward from home to the

Cancer Centre for treatment. First of these was that she wasn't able to give the two boys the attention she would have liked. It was hard lying up in bed listening to Paul talking to them, or sit in a chair in the living room and watch them playing with one another, having the continual inclination, but never the energy, to interact with them herself.

Her other concern was the housework. She wasn't able to cook, clean, wash and iron as once she did. Ali pushed herself to try and continue with the cooking, but it was a struggle. In other areas, though, she just had to sit back and allow others to help. Paul took charge of the washing, ironing and cleaning. Lawson brought in supplies and a team of ladies from Glenabbey kept arriving at the door with delicious pre-cooked meals.

By the middle of the third week, when Ali was really beginning to feel the intense strain of the constant treatment, a system of care had become established.

Although finding Ali's illness emotionally hard to handle, the members of Glenabbey had no difficulty responding practically to the situation. They came round to visit the Watson home with a dual aim. Reason number one was to enquire about Ali and assure all of them 'they were remembering them in prayer,' with the second being to present Paul with 'something to put in the freezer.' This was often a specially, and no doubt lovingly, prepared meal, 'just ready to pop into the microwave.'

Paul and Ali were touched by such an organised commitment to kindness. On one occasion, when Paul had come in from trying to find space in the freezer for yet another practical and generous token of prayerful concern, he remarked to Ali, "I think the first two recipes in any twenty-first century church cookbook must be lasagne or chicken and broccoli bake."

This brought a smile to Ali's face before she replied with a mild chastening, "You shouldn't say that Paul. It sounds so ungrateful."

"Believe me, I'm certainly not ungrateful," he assured her at once. "What I said was not out of criticism but appreciation. Everybody is so kind!"

God, through His children, had taken complete control of their feeding programme.

With such a dedicated back-up team behind them Paul and Ali made it through the six weeks. Mondays were special nights of togetherness. They usually began with Paul seeing Ali settled into the ward in preparation for her chemo before setting out on the 'pizza run.' When this had been shared and eaten Paul drew a chair up beside his wife's bed and they talked and watched TV together. What they tried to ignore was the constant drip of hopefully-healing drugs into Ali's arm and the 'beep-beep-bo!' of the alarms that were constantly sounding round the ward. This was a warning system to alert the nurses that an intravenous line was blocked and there always seemed to be one going off within earshot!

On the final Friday of radiotherapy the lady oncologist, who had been supervising the programme throughout, gave Paul and Ali an appointment for six weeks away. That took them into the middle of May and was when they would do further tests to gauge how successful the treatment had been.

Another period of waiting ensued but this time it was good for it allowed Ali time to relax, build up strength, and as she did so enjoy working with the boys. When the day of their review appointment came, and the examinations and tests were conducted, the news was good.

"We are pleased to say that the tumour appears to have gone away," was the oncologist's final summing up of the position. "We will be calling you back for check-ups periodically, but in the meantime things are looking promising."

Paul and Ali were over the moon. They could barely wait to get home to tell Ali's dad, Peter and Niky and their attentive Christian friends from Glenabbey. It was such exciting, emancipating news. They felt so relieved. So free. The cloud that had been hanging over them for six months had lifted and dispersed.

They were full of praise for the excellent medical care they had received. In their elation they didn't really take time to recognise that there was a Supreme Power at work in their lives, however, directing their every movement and the medical team's every decision. They had prayed to God passionately often during the period but omitted to return and thank Him for the positive answer.

Paul and Ali were liberated now. Free and ready to pick up where they had left off, and just get on with the rest of their lives.

Now that Ali was feeling better she expressed a vision she had been cultivating during the confining and debilitating days of treatment. It had kept her going, and the time had come to share it with Paul.

"I would love to go travelling again, only this time with the boys," she said.

That would be no problem to Paul. He was thrilled that she felt well enough to even contemplate such a venture, and to have Mark and Euan with them would be a wonderful bonus.

"I think it could be arranged!" he assured her.

CHAPTER 11
WHERE'S MY LOLLIPOP?

It was arranged, easily and eagerly, for September.

Paul returned to work after Ali's reassuring news, and she in turn was delighted to resume the role of full-time mum. She considered it a wonderful privilege to be able to enjoy the boys without the worry or the weakness that had been an integral part of her life for the first five months of the year.

A family friend had offered Paul and Ali the use of their apartment in the south of France, and the young parents were so grateful for this and opted to make use of it in September. They were able to leave it until after the school holiday months as the boys were both pre-school age, and reasoned that Ali should be fully fit by then.

Paul and Ali were experienced world-travellers but this holiday was to prove different from any trip they had ever taken before, and even more special. When going abroad in their younger days they only had their own needs and preferences to think about. Now, though, they were happy to view everything from a totally different perspective. What, they kept asking themselves, could they do to help their two little sons appreciate the adventure of travel?

The initial thrill for Mark and Euan was the flight from Belfast to Nice. They had never been on a plane before and the thought of it had them both hugely excited.

Among the many well-considered provisions the parents made for their two boys was to bring a supply of 'lollipops for their ears.' Mark was a little confused at first when he heard his mum and dad discussing this. Any lollipops he had ever had up until then he had put in his mouth. Why would you want to stick a lollipop in your ear? When it was explained to him that sucking 'a lolly' during take-off would save him having any problems with his ears it all made some kind of sense. Euan, being so much younger, didn't have any such hang-ups. A lollipop was a lollipop and if someone gave you one you put in your mouth and enjoyed it, no questions asked!

On arrival in Nice Paul collected their hire car, loaded it with suitcases, a buggy and a travel cot and they set off to locate the holiday apartment which was to become the family home for the next two weeks. The boys found the two hour drive along the beautiful south coast of France quite tiring after a while. Paul and Ali kept their spirits up by talking about the places they had visited last time they were there. That though, was a world apart from this experience. They had been camping last time, and there had just been the two of them. Now they were heading for a luxury apartment with their two precious boys, whose occasional questions and quaint comments helped them see everything they had thought familiar in an entirely new light, as they drove along.

The final leg of the journey took them down from the mountains and out to the coast to Cavalaire-sur-Mer, the seaside town in which the apartment was located. Switching from the confinement of the car to the freedom of the apartment saw the boys suddenly tap into a hidden reserve of energy. They dashed from room to room with excited whoops, then out onto the balcony and back in again repeatedly, as their mum and dad endeavoured to perform such mundane tasks as unpacking cases, putting up a travel cot and writing a shopping list.

Before setting off to explore the holiday attractions of the town Paul and Ali had to bring the boys along on a stocking-up shopping trip. They had been told where the nearest supermarket was and now it was a question of what do they have that the boys will eat? The selection was fine and they were soon returning with a number of bags to unload into the fridge and kitchen cupboards.

Now it was time for the holiday to begin, in earnest.

First stop, on what was left of what had been an extremely

busy day, was the beach. Mark and Euan could hardly wait to get down on to the sand and run in and out of the warm water of the Mediterranean as it rippled in tiny waves on to the shore. It was great, and the thrilling thing was there were other little sandy coves close by and two weeks in which to visit every single one of them, stretching out ahead.

This was the life!

Or was it?

There was another aspect of the holiday in that luxury apartment to which Ali and Paul had particularly looked forward. It was having their two tired-but-happy little sons safely tucked up and fast asleep in bed allowing them to sit with a quiet drink on the balcony with the sights and sounds of a balmy night providing the ultimate in relaxation therapy.

That wasn't how it turned out on the first night, however.

The parents' plan was that the boys would share the twin room, Mark in a bed and Euan in his cot, allowing them to have the double room. Sounded simple and sensible to them. The frustrating thing was that it sounded both simple and sensible to the boys, too. But for an entirely different reason!

It allowed them to chat, giggle and make funny noises. This went on for ages. The trouble was they were not only keeping each other amused, but they were also keeping each other awake!

Paul and Ali solved the problem by moving Mark into their double bed and they ended up spending that, and each succeeding night sleeping on two single sofa beds in the living room. It was a small sacrifice to make for the joy of being able to be on holiday and having the boys with them. And they got to sit on the balcony for as long as they liked, chatting and recalling the highlights of the day, every night from then on!

Most of the next week was spent exploring a succession of cove beaches in the area. Paul and the boys built sandcastles and Ali, who loved swimming in the sea, was in her element. There was something for everyone and the days seemed to pass in a sun-blessed sea-cooled blur.

On the two days they were able to tear themselves away from the beach, 'just to try something different for a change,' they made car trips up to and through a number of non-too-distant unspoilt mountain villages. This was probably more interesting for mum and dad than for Mark and Euan for the rewards were good – and tasty! In many of the new places they visited they would have a stop to cool off, and sample the local speciality in ice-cream. Delicious!

The weather was so good they ate most meals alfresco and the boys loved nothing better than to share their parents' passion for pizza at some open air location. One of the family favourite spots for this kind of outdoor eating was the marina. There always seemed to be something interesting going on there, something to chat about as they ate. On one special evening they had ordered a take away pizza but hadn't asked for it to be cut into portions before leaving the pizzeria. What were they going to do? The boys were intrigued as Paul produced the Swiss army knife he always carried with him and used it to slice up both the pizza and the base of the box as well! It was a tranquil summer evening and they sat together long after the pizza was finished and the shredded box binned, watching the sun send a shaft of orange light across the sea. When this disappeared, followed by the sun itself behind a low bank of cloud, the sky turned a blazing-flame colour, before giving way to the darkness.

Only then did the Watson family decide it was time to return to the apartment, with bed for the boys, and balcony for the parents.

At the start of the second week of their holiday Paul, Ali and the boys met an English couple and their daughter Charlotte, on the beach. Both couples, and the children, were glad of the company, all for diverse, but nonetheless positive, reasons.

For Mark and 'Lottie' it was 'love at first sight!' They were inseparable from the moment of first meeting. Both sets of parents were amused to see and hear the little blonde girl with the prim south-of-England accent and the three-year old boy from County Antrim, chatting away as if they had known each other for all of their short lifetimes, totally oblivious to all that was going on around them.

The women's friendship strengthened as they shared memories of hospital experiences. Lyn had to remain in hospital for a period because of complications following Charlotte's birth. Ali had plenty to share after her extended hospitalisation earlier in the year. And even when they had exhausted medical matters they were never short of a subject for conversation. The recollection of the early rearing, and observation of the current antics of the children, presented an unending source of topics.

Paul and James talked away about everything and anything as they threw themselves into in the design and construction challenge of the holiday. The building of sandcastles! The two men spent their time building huge castles on the beach. They were of course, 'for the children.' The strange thing about it was, however, that they seemed to get a bigger kick out of engaging in a light-hearted rivalry in comparing their handiwork, than the children did in viewing them. The three kids fetched stones, shells, feathers and driftwood for final embellishment when asked, but otherwise generally enjoyed the freedom of 'doing their own thing!'

Euan appreciated meeting Lottie too. It wasn't for love of her, particularly, but for love of what she had. Lottie had come on holiday complete with a portable DVD player and a vast selection of children's DVD's. This meant that when Euan fancied a change from the restless round of activity he could catch up with a bit of essential viewing!

Everyone enjoyed the days spent together and they were all sad when it came time to go home. Lottie and her mum and dad left a day earlier than the Watson family as they were motoring up through France to make the Channel crossing. It felt so empty for a few hours after they left but they were soon out again relishing the freedom from work pressures for Paul and the absence of hospital appointments for Ali.

Paul, Ali and the boys were up early on the day they were to fly back to Belfast. They had to drive to the airport and return the hire car before booking in for the flight. No one seemed to mind the trip back. They had so much to think about and talk about.

When seated on board the plane Ali gave the boys each 'a lollipop for his ears.' These were happily sucked for takeoff, but the flight hadn't progressed far northward over France until Euan was sound asleep, his lolly hanging out of his mouth at a crazy angle. Paul removed it for him, wrapping it in a piece of its original cellophane, to keep, in case he woke up. He didn't. It had been an early start, and the little boy was exhausted.

They were preparing for the descent into Belfast when Ali nudged Euan gently to stir him awake. Gradually coming to, he asked, in an assertive tone for one still so sleepy, "Where's my lollipop?"

Paul, Ali and Mark laughed heartily at his concern and the sticky confection was replaced in the mouth from which it had been removed. The shared laughter summed up the effect the holiday had on all four of them. It had been a wonderful, carefree fortnight.

Lawson met them at the airport and drove them home, with the boys taking turns to tell him about everything from Lottie to the apartment, from sandcastles on the beach to their favourite flavour of ice-cream!

The memory of that holiday was to become extremely precious to the young couple too, in the days ahead. Paul returned to work, and Ali slipped effortlessly back into her daily routine.

All seemed blissfully normal.

Then came yet another head-on collision with reality...

CHAPTER 12

THE BAD NEWS ROOM

In mid-November Ali became aware of a small lump in her groin. She talked to Paul about it. Surely it couldn't be anything more sinister than a hernia this time, they kept telling themselves. The cancer was gone wasn't it?

When Ali mentioned her concern about this to her GP she in turn referred her back to the Cancer Centre. 'Just to have it checked out.'

Ali had two appointments at the end of the month, and on Thursday 6 December attended for a third. Assuming this to be yet another routine scan Paul left for work as usual and Ali drove up to the City Hospital alone.

It was just after midday when Paul took a phone call at his desk. At first there seemed to be no one there. Then came a faint voice he recognised as Ali's. She was sobbing and that was making speaking difficult. "It's not good, Paul," he heard. He tried to ask questions but his wife's replies were so tearful they were incoherent.

After a few more emotional moments another voice came on the line. Paul recognised it immediately. It was that of the radiotherapy practitioner they both knew from previous painful experience. "Paul, could you possibly get down here?" she enquired "We would like to speak to you both."

"No problem," he replied, sensing instantly that something was gravely amiss. "I'll be there straightaway."

Paul replaced the receiver and turned to a colleague with the colour draining rapidly from his face. "It's back!" he croaked.

Having been given permission to 'go and be with her,' Paul

made another dash from his base in Lisburn Road Police Station to the Cancer Centre at the City Hospital, with his head spinning. Last time he had done that trip, having received an urgent summons, it had been to be with his mother-in-law. This time it was potentially even more serious. It was his wife.

The radiotherapist had told Paul the room they were in but he didn't need directions to find it. They had all been in there together just over ten months before. After that experience in late January Paul and Ali had nicknamed it 'the bad news room.' Was it about to live up to its reputation? From what he had been able to understand of what he had been able to make out of the telephone call with his distressed wife, he had a suspicion that it might just be going to.

And he was right.

Arriving into 'the bad news room' Paul found three ladies waiting for him. One was the consultant oncologist, another the radiotherapist who had phoned him and the third was Ali. She was sitting with an elbow on a small table, and when she looked up her eyes were brimming with tears.

In such a sombre atmosphere no one really needed to say anything, but someone did. It was Ali. "It's back!" she whispered.

The oncologist explained that the recent tests had revealed another tumour and they would be holding a meeting later in the month to determine the most appropriate course of chemotherapy to treat it. There was further upsetting news, too. The drugs used in this more intensive treatment, the first dose of which they had already 'pencilled in' to be administered on 28 December, would cause hair loss.

As on previous occasions the understanding medical practitioners allowed Paul and Ali as much time as they needed to come to terms with these distressing developments. When they felt sufficiently composed to face the world again, and just as they were about to leave, the oncologist gave Paul a handwritten note, remarking as she did so, "You will need that."

It was to his employers stating that from the end of December he would require to be off work indefinitely. That did little to lift their spirits on the way home.

There was little conversation in the car. Just tears. It was back to shock and awe, heartbreak and heartache. Where did they go from here? How would they ever start to tell everybody once more?

They had just over three weeks before Ali was due to return to the Cancer Centre for her first course of chemo. That gave Paul and Ali precisely 22 days to look at and wonder about the boys and their future and put the family and their close friends in the picture for a second traumatic time. When not engaged in these activities they had time to pray, reflect and struggle to come to terms with the situation emotionally and make sense of it spiritually.

One source of relief and diversionary focus was the fact that Christmas was coming. The pre- 'bad news room' plan had been for Paul, Ali and the boys to visit Ali's sister Janet, her husband Doug and their little son Iain in Gairloch, Scotland, over Christmas. Paul had already rented the same idyllic seaside cottage they had stayed in on a short holiday to Gairloch earlier in the year. On hearing Ali's news, the cottage booking was cancelled and Doug and Janet arranged instead to come to Northern Ireland to be with Paul, Ali and family.

Doug, who was an accomplished cook, said, "Don't worry. We will do Christmas at your house!" Assuring Paul and Ali they didn't 'need to worry about a thing,' he took charge of all the arrangements for the Christmas dinner. They were quite happy to leave it to him, amidst all their more pressing concerns, and what a wonderful job he made of it.

On Christmas Eve morning a Tesco delivery van arrived outside the Watson home and delivered bag after bag of Christmas fare in preparation for the next day. Doug had ordered online all he would require to put on a first-class Christmas dinner! He soon put them all to work preparing sprouts, peeling potatoes or stirring bread sauce. The busyness of the day helped everyone forget why they were now in Greenisland and not Gairloch.

Christmas morning was a rewarding time for Paul and Ali as they watched the wide-eyed wonder of their two boys as they tore the paper from their presents and opened them. Ali had always maintained that Mark and Euan would not be 'spoilt' by having so much they would not really appreciate anything, but rather satisfied with having sufficient to allow them to appreciate everything. And as the lovingly-wrapped, colourful parcels were opened one by one it turned out just as she had wished.

After breakfast it was off to the Christmas morning service in Glenabbey. It was a friendly, family-focused service with children taking part in the celebration of the birth of the Saviour. On the way out Ali was surrounded by concerned friends wishing her 'all the best for Friday,' and assuring her, amid hugs and kisses, that they would be 'praying for her every day.'

Back at home Doug and Janet took over. They had accompanied Lawson to the service in Greenisland Presbyterian Church and when they arrived at Paul and Ali's house they set to work. Mark and Euan shared their toys with cousin Iain, Lawson and Margaret relaxed, and Paul and Ali enjoyed sharing in the boys' fun. All they had to do was answer a few 'where would we find?' questions from the self-appointed chef and his assistant.

After what amounted to little short of a mediaeval banquet it was back to party games and party hats. It was clear that although each of the adults had his or her personal misgivings about what lay ahead they were all determined to make that Christmas day a memorable one for the children. When it came late in the evening, and after Lawson had taken all the visitors home, Paul and Ali prepared their two boys for bed.

Their excited conversation, followed by a drift into an exhausted sleep of contentment, afforded the gratified parents the pleasure of knowing that, regardless of their own growing apprehension, Mark and Euan had loved their Christmas Day.

Thursday 27 December was Paul and Ali's sixth wedding anniversary and the occasion was noted and mutually appreciated rather than openly celebrated.

Doug and Janet came around to be with them that evening and they shared a meal together. It was strange but the conversation was all to do with past recollection rather than future anticipation. They looked back on Paul and Ali's wedding day, recounting some of the outstanding incidents, then switched to talking about their jobs, their children, their churches, their homes and even their cars. It was shallow conversation for it was obvious that nobody was talking about what he or she was thinking about.

Days long past and Christmas just past were easy to discuss. Ali's condition and what lay ahead were not. 'Tomorrow' was lying heavily on everyone's mind.

When Doug and Janet left Paul and Ali talked and prayed well into the night.

What would tomorrow and the days, weeks and months ahead hold for Ali as a person and a patient, and for her husband and family?

CHAPTER 13

AM I SICK ENOUGH?

For six blissful months God had permitted Ali to forget what it was like to be in constant pain. What it was like to be helplessly weak and continually nauseous.

She went for her first course of chemo the following day as scheduled and soon all the old sickening sensations were back. After attending for the second session on January 18 2008 Ali returned to feeling totally wiped-out. Paul and she had known from previous experience what to expect but that didn't make it any easier to deal with. The oncologist had been right in her observation when giving Paul that note. He did 'need that.' He certainly had to be off work to organise the boys and care for Ali all day every day.

The main difference from the previous treatment was the predicted loss of Ali's shock of red hair. Ali worried terribly about this, not particularly about herself or how she would look, but more for Paul's sake, and how he would react. She knew he loved her hair, for he couldn't possibly have been lying all those times he had told her so. One day, when her flame-coloured locks had started to drop out in handfuls, she said to him. "Look how quickly my hair is coming out, Paul."

"Don't worry about it, Ali," her husband consoled. "Sure mine is coming out too!"

He was right. It was, but a lot less perceptibly than his wife's. They had a laugh about it, and Ali was obviously relieved to have shared her concerns with him. From then on they accepted it as a fact of life and never needed to consider it a problem again.

Towards the end of January, Ali began writing a private journal. This allowed her to jot down her innermost thoughts relating mostly to her emotional and spiritual strengths and struggles. As the trying days of her treatment came and went, making her feel drained and dreadful, this volume was to quickly become a release valve for pent-up personal responses. As it progressed she came to use it as a means to express her faith in God and her appreciation of the loving care lavished on her by both her natural and Christian families.

The first entries in that journal were both Scripture verses which had obviously encouraged her as she looked ahead into the unknown...

26th January 08

Jeremiah 30 v 17 *But I will restore you to health and heal your wounds, declares the Lord.*

Jer. 31 v 3 *I have loved you with an everlasting love; I have drawn you with loving kindness.*

The next day's entry showed how Ali began to strive for an acceptable mind-set to help address her difficult position...

27th January 08

I'm sure the pain is getting less. I want to be positive but not set myself up for disappointment.
Must continue to pray for healing – not acceptance and resignation.
Last time I put my faith in the doctors and their course of treatment – and thanked God for it.
This time I'm starting to understand what it is to really put my faith in God – it is for Him to heal me.

In addition to commencing writing her journal Ali had another very practical matter to consider towards the end of her first month of treatment. Ali's dad had told her that he was planning to remarry on February 7. He had developed a friendship with Christine, a lovely widow, and Lawson asked Ali if she would act as a witness to the wedding ceremony.

His daughter was delighted to accept this invitation as it would provide an alternative focus to tablets, treatment and tiredness, but she had some special matters to take into account. There are two things a women is usually fussy about when attending a wedding, not to mention actually taking part in one, her hair and her outfit. In Ali's case both these issues would require careful, even super-sensitive, consideration.

The chemo drugs had caused her to lose her hair and the steroids had led to a gain in weight.

First to be addressed was the question of the hair. The Cancer Centre arranged for Ali to attend a special facility provided by Macmillan Cancer Care, where she could have a personal wig crafted to her precise requirements. Paul and she went together and were soon engrossed in proceedings as a competent and caring stylist produced a series of different colours and lengths of wig for Ali to try.

When they had created the new hair image the lady who had helped Ali decide on it presented her with another option. She produced a number of colourful headscarves and taught Ali how best to fix them on securely to give attractive cover without the danger of falling or blowing off, embarrassingly.

By the time Paul and Ali left the centre well over an hour later they were carrying a bag containing a carefully and perfectly fashioned wig and two of the headscarves Ali had most fancied. Problem number one, that of what to do about the hair, was solved. The challenge of acquiring a suitable outfit was all that now remained. .

Ali's Aunt Margaret gave her a present of enough money to buy 'something for the wedding.' Thus raising sufficient funds wasn't something she needed to worry about, but finding a suitable outfit was to prove more difficult.

As was frequently the case Aunt Margaret offered to look after the boys to allow Paul and Ali to go shopping, but their first expedition to the shops turned out to be something of a disaster. They thought, to avoid having to walk long distances, they would go to an out-of-town shopping centre. Here Ali tried on a number of items but any of the few things she thought she liked just wouldn't fit.

Eventually she came out of a shop in tears. "I'm fat, Paul, and I'll never get clothes to fit me!" she sobbed in disappointment and frustration. "I'm just not going to be able to find anything to wear! What are we going to do? I'm going to let dad down!"

Recognising that the emotional upset of this experience, combined with utter physical weakness, was in danger of triggering an all-systems collapse, Paul suggested what he considered the most appropriate course of action.

"What about just giving it up for today and going home," he proposed. "We can always try somewhere else another day when you are feeling better."

Ali had no quarrel with that idea, so they went home, and when she was feeling up to it a few days later, visited Belfast city centre. Paul drew Ali's attention to a skirt he thought she might like in a shop in Royal Avenue, but neither of them could decide 'what would go with it.'

A shop assistant's question, "Can I help you with anything there?" was exactly what they needed to hear, and they showed her the skirt, asking if she had 'anything that would match it.' Within minutes that young woman, who was simply doing her job, had become something of 'a star' in the couple's eyes.

She was obviously a sensitive person, and probably recognised from Ali's appearance and headscarf that this wasn't her 'normal customer', and served her with appropriate sympathetic attention. Her caring attitude paid off too, for by the time she had finished her trips to and from the fitting-room Ali had been completely 'kitted out' for the wedding! Her sole concern now was about how she would be feeling when her dad's 'big day' came.

Thursday 7 February was the day of the wedding which Ali attended as planned wearing one of her headscarves and her new 'rig-out,' and acted as a witness to the marriage, in accordance with her dad's wish. The service was held in Greenisland Presbyterian Church with the reception afterwards in Malone House, and this brought back happy memories for Paul and Ali. An added bonus for them both was that they now had their two little boys there with them, enjoying the freedom to run around in the spacious surroundings, and thinking it very funny that mummy and daddy were all dressed up!

Although exhausted at the end of the day, from the physical exertion of actually being there and the mental agitation of coping with the kind enquiries and sincerely expressed good wishes of family friends, she enjoyed the experience. The hugely gratifying thing about it all was that when she arrived home to go straight to bed for a well earned rest Ali had the satisfaction of knowing that her dad was happy the day had gone so well.

The following day Ali went for another course of chemotherapy and then on Saturday 9 February she attended a healing service in the Waterfront Hall, Belfast. Paul had seen it advertised and Ali didn't think she would be well enough to go, but amazingly she was.

As Paul and she sat together towards the end of the service an announcement was made asking anyone who wished 'to be prayed' for to come out to the front.

As some began leaving their seats to make their way forward Ali turned to Paul and asked, "Do you think I should go down? Am I sick enough?"

Paul looked across at her in admiration, although he was slightly baffled by her reticence.

This was Ali wearing a headscarf from hair loss through cancer treatment.

This was Ali with the bloated body from the use of steroid drugs.

This was Ali who was often in terrible pain.

And she was asking, "Am I sick enough?!"

"Don't be silly, Ali! I think you are somehow!" her husband assured her. He was touched by her humility, always thinking of others ahead of herself, but was nonetheless quite sure there would be few going forward in any more need of healing than she was.

That word of encouragement was all Ali needed to make her leave her seat and join the others already assembling at the front of the arena.

The lead up to, followed by her reaction to, the experience of that evening is best described in her journal entry of a few days later, when she wrote...

12th February 08

Last Tues on the way home from hosp we passed an advertisement for a healing service in the W'front on Sat night. All I saw was the date – couldn't go, day after chemo. But Paul saw it was David Carr – he wrote the foreword to Sharon McKay's book. It seemed clear that we should try to go.

David Carr anointed me with oil and prayed briefly. Then a lady came and prayed with me – that I may have life over death and that my tumours would shrivel and shrink. She had no way of knowing what was wrong with me. I am encouraged that I am praying for healing within God's will.

Ali lived in the strength of her faith and in the knowledge that her family and friends were praying for her persistently for a further two weeks and more until she attended the Cancer Centre for an appointment on Thursday 28 February. That was when she heard some news that dented her confidence for a bit. She shared her thoughts about it in her journal a few days later, when she wrote...

3rd March 08

28th Feb. Chemo not working – have to see if surgery or different chemo are possible.

Psalm 30

Vs 2 'O Lord my God, I called to you for help and you healed me,'

Vs 9 'What gain is there in my destruction?'

If David can question God like this – so can I...

CHAPTER 14

STEP FORWARD IN FAITH

While questioning sets of circumstances can sometimes be disturbing and acceptance of them difficult, occasional breaks in routine can often produce a positive effect.

It was in an effort to provide such an alternative to down days and bad news that Aunt Margaret offered to keep the boys for a few hours on the morning of Tuesday 4 March. This left Paul and Ali free to go out for breakfast together, a welcome treat.

When in the restaurant something happened which encouraged Ali, showing her, if not Christian charity, then certainly practical care and concern. Two days later she recorded it in her journal, and was obviously most appreciative...

6th March 08 (Thursday)
On Tues we went to Papa Brown's and had a lovely morning. When we went to pay someone had already paid! Two ladies at the next table. We didn't know them. I didn't even see them...'

On the Saturday and Sunday immediately following that entry Paul and Ali had two of their University friends over from Scotland for a visit. Murray and Kristy were upset to see Ali bloated by drugs and wearing her headscarf as a result of her cancer treatment. There were some laughs but more tears as the two couples shared what had been happening in all of their lives from they last had been together.

Since Ali was feeling very weak and just wanted to stay in bed, the four friends spent most of the time in the bedroom. A king-size bed, with Ali at one side of it, formed a makeshift 'picnic table,' for the meals. They had a 'Chinese' on the first evening and a Thai curry the next. It was tempting to think it was 'just like old times' back in Aberdeen, but all four of them were acutely aware that it wasn't.

Meeting up with their friends had been great but parting on Sunday night was hard for them all. Ali's spirits had been lifted by the effort Murray and Kristy had made to come, and especially by the symbol of hope Kristy had brought. The visiting friend had no idea of the meaning of what she had been asked to deliver, or that Ali would be able to attach any particular significance to it. The sick young mother did, because she had received 'a prayer cloth' from David Carr in the post a few days earlier. Summing up the weekend in words Ali wrote...

Murray and Kristy came over for the w'end. Kristy gave me a handkerchief from a colleague – all she knew was it was 'anointed' – it came in an envelope with a post-it note saying 'Acts 19. 12.'

Everything points to healing!! This woman didn't know I was praying for healing or that I would understand what she was sending me – this can only be the work of God.

An entry a few days later catalogued her outstanding commitment to God and His will for her. Her physical pain was increasing and natural strength decreasing, despite being surrounded by prayer and the deep love of her husband and family, and being afforded excellent medical attention. Probably after having read in the book of Daniel in the Bible as part of a personal study, she wrote...

12th March 08
Daniel 3. 19 – 27
Praise God in the midst of the fire and see what your God can do.

Shadrach, Meshach and Abednego said 'if we are thrown into the blazing furnace, the God we serve is able to deliver us from it, and He will rescue us from your hand, O king. But even if He does not, we want you to know, O king, that we will not serve your gods or worship the image of gold you have set up.'

They believed in God's power to save them but acknowledged His sovereignty – the decision is God's.

God is glorified by how you act in the fire. Why does God not instantly free / heal you? So that He can step into the fire with you.

People see how you act in your suffering. Be sure it is to the glory of God.

Step forward in faith and believe – but remember God is sovereign, and the ultimate outcome is His will / His decision.

On Friday 21ˢᵗ March, Paul, Ali and the two boys went to spend the Easter weekend on the north coast. Their friends Brian and Andrea Duff had a house in Portrush and kindly offered the Watson family the use of it over the weekend. Ali didn't know, when Brian and Andrea first mentioned it to them, whether or not she would be well enough to go. Her determination to appear 'normal', despite both pain and discomfort, however, saw her into the car with her husband and two excited little boys that afternoon.

On Saturday morning Paul took Ali to Coleraine for a specific purpose, which she recorded briefly in her journal, recalling...

In Portrush for Easter weekend. Went to Coleraine on Sat. morning. The Vineyard Church have a healing ministry on Sat mornings so I went for prayer. 3 women (inc. Ann) prayed powerfully that the cancer would leave my body....

That afternoon Paul and Ali brought the boys to Barry's Amusement Park in Portrush and when there they met friends from Glenabbey. Andy and Nicola and Peter and Sarah-Ann were spending the weekend in caravans in the area with their children. Mark and Euan were soon playing around Barry's with their friends from home. Realising how happy the children were to be together Paul and Ali invited everyone round to the house where they were staying.

Ali had become close friends with Nicola and Sarah-Ann, having met them some time before at MOPs (Mothers of Preschoolers) in Glenabbey, and so they had plenty to talk about. The men knew each other also and when the adults all decided it would be a good idea to share tea together Andy volunteered to go out and buy fish and chips.

It was a wonderful, if somewhat impromptu, time of sharing with the children not very sure whether to eat or to play was more important, and their mums and dads chatting away informally. The visiting couples were acutely conscious of Ali's condition, recognising that she was probably 'putting on a brave face', for them all.

She was, too. There came a point, though, when Ali had to excuse herself, as the pain had become so bad she felt her only recourse to any kind of relief was to lie down in bed. The others then dispersed towards their separate caravans, leaving Paul and Ali to reflect on what had been a very pleasant, though never for Ali pain free, day.

Next morning the family attended the Vineyard Church in Coleraine, where they met Ann again. She encouraged Ali, telling her she believed she would be healed. The boys enjoyed their visit too, not for anything that was said, but for the fact they were each given an Easter egg!

On Easter Monday Paul parked at Portballintrae and the four of them walked along the coastal path to the world-famous Giant's Causeway. Ali found the going difficult, but the joy she experienced seeing the look of wonder on her sons' faces as the local tourist steam train passed them on its way to the Causeway, and then watching the steam belch from it in the 'station' there, helped compensate for her effort in agony.

When they arrived home in Greenisland after their much-appreciated Easter break Ali's pain became excruciating. On learning of this the palliative care specialists in the Cancer Centre in the City Hospital referred her to the Hospice at Home service.

When Sue, a very caring nurse with the service, began to call out to see Ali and assess her condition she realised she would be unable to manage her new patient's pain with the resources available to her. The only solution she could suggest was for Ali to be admitted to the Northern Ireland Hospice, where stronger, and hopefully more effective drugs than she was permitted to prescribe, could be administered.

Ali resisted the idea at first. She felt that going into the Hospice had an air of finality about it. What would everybody think when they heard? Was there not a general perception that people only went in there to die?

She expressed these misgivings to Sue on one of her regular visits and the experienced nurse, who had come across that misperception so many times before, was able to reassure her. Sue endeavoured to set Ali's mind at ease by explaining that the Hospice, as an institution, existed as a centre for symptom relief and pain management. She then went on to spell out gently something which her patient knew only too well. The intensity of the pain she was enduring made her an eminently suitable candidate for the level of care it could provide.

As Ali struggled to come to terms with the prospect of becoming an in-patient at the Hospice, her pain became almost unbearable. Paul found it distressing to watch his wife, the woman he loved, in such extreme agony, and when Sue phoned him on Tuesday, 15 April with an offer, he accepted without hesitation.

"Paul, we have a bed in the Hospice for Ali. Will she take it?" she wanted to know.

"Yes, she will. She needs to be in with you now," was the husband and carer's immediate response.

Ali didn't raise any objections, either. Her mental struggle with supposed stigma was all behind her. By then she had reached the point where her physical pain was dictating the big decisions.

She was genuinely relieved to be admitted to a room of her own in the Northern Ireland Hospice that evening.

Her journal entry two days later revealed her continued steadfast faith in God despite her deteriorating condition and change of location...

Thursday 17th April   *(In Hospice)*

Matt 21 vs. 22
If you believe, you will receive whatever you ask for in prayer.

I pray that God would heal me in Jesus' name. I know that He can and so I pray that He will...

CHAPTER 15

A GOD MOMENT

There were only five single rooms in the Hospice and Ali had been allocated one of them. This was for a very sound medical reason. She was to have continued chemotherapy and the risk of infection would be minimised in a separate room.

The advantage of this was that Paul could come in, and bring the boys in, to visit at any time. It also gave Ali an opportunity to ponder her entire situation, and the chance to entertain, and be encouraged by, other visitors from her natural and church families, in private, when they called.

Three days after her admission to the Hospice Ali's written recollection recorded the roller-coaster of emotions she could experience within the course of a single twelve-hour period. These were mostly related to spiritual considerations as she reflected on issues like God's word to her, His presence with her and His provision for her...

Friday 18th *(Hospice)*

Today I had a blood transfusion and was trapped in my room for most of the day.

I met the chaplain this morning. We talked about healing – he doesn't believe in the 'name it and claim it' school of thought and thinks suggesting if you have enough faith you will be healed is almost cruel. He prayed that God would meet me at the point of my need.

Went for a walk after the transfusion and talked to God about the verses I'd received and asked how they all fit in and if I can apply them to me. Was struggling to claim any verses for myself. Prayed for a sign or word to help.

Laura Taggart and her mum Stella came to visit. A real gift from God. They talked about God wanting the best for us, wanting to heal, etc. Stella had this verse for me

Isaiah 43 vs. 1-3 (Living Bible)

'But now the Lord who created you, O Israel says, "Don't be afraid for I have ransomed you; I have called you by my name; you are mine. When you go through deep waters and great trouble I will be with you. When you go through rivers of difficulty you will not drown. When you walk through the fire of oppression you will not be burned up; the flames will not consume you. For I am the Lord your God, the Holy One of Israel, your Saviour..."'

I showed Stella the verses in Jeremiah 30 and 31, I have been given. She says if they have been given to me as a word from God, I can hold onto them.

Ruth in the room next door is a Christian. We first met in the Cancer Centre in 2007 – Feb maybe. She read me a verse from Hosea – must find out what. We prayed together for God's peace.

Recognising that Ruth was in the room next to Ali helped Paul handle the problem of parting in the evenings. The management had offered Paul a bed to allow him to remain in with his wife but he was unable to as he was anxious to keep life as normal as possible for Mark and Euan. Knowing that Ali and Ruth would meet in either of their rooms to chat and pray together after he left allowed him to go away with a slightly lighter heart. Although worried about Ali's physical condition, he was always thankful for the company she had.

Ruth was a gentle Christian lady, a long-term cancer patient, and undoubtedly a gift from God to both Paul and Ali.

Although she had only been in the Hospice a few days Ali found her first short visit home very difficult. The Hospice had become her haven. Pain-killing drugs were available there, and she knew she was only a bell-push away from expert medical care. A brief diary summary on her return recalled the emotional trauma of the experience...

Saturday 19th
Went home – really struggled – went down to Dad's – cried - just couldn't cope.

Despite the 'downer' she had lived through that day Paul called and took her out again to a prayer group on Sunday afternoon. Ali was glad to be meeting with a number of her 'prayer partners' again and her delight at being with them was matched by the genuine thrill it gave them to have her sitting among them once more.

When recording the afternoon's events later that evening, when back in her room, she wrote...

Sunday 20th
We went to Andrea and David Moore's for tea. First meeting of our wee prayer group. Really encouraging to meet and share with other couples. God gave me a couple of pain free hours to enjoy. Yet another answer to prayer.

What she didn't mention, though, was that when it came her turn to pray Ali prayed only for others, and not herself. Her friends were amazed at this. They had been pitying her and praying for her with great feeling, but she prayed only for them and for needs they had told her about in the church.

Nor had she lost her sense of humour, for as she was praying there appeared to be some kind of altercation among the group of children in the room next door. Euan's voice could be heard, screaming his point rather forcefully. Ali interrupted the flow of her prayer to interject a specific and urgent plea.

"And Lord, please don't let Euan murder anybody while we are praying!" she begged.

When Paul was taking her back to the Hospice a short time later Ali remarked to him, "That was wonderful, Paul. Just to see everyone again. And what I can hardly believe is that for all the time I was in there I was free of pain. Surely that can only be the hand of God."

The joy of the afternoon was replaced later, in her mind, by a sense of reality creeping in, a growing personal concern about her worsening condition. This, in turn, was offset by an assurance from the Scriptures.

Before retiring to try for a few hours of drugs-permitting sleep, Ali made her final journal entry for the day. Still under Sun 20th she revealed...

I am praying tonight for God's peace as I go to hosp. for chemo tomorrow. I think these tumours are growing – have to talk to oncologist. Praying for strength to get through that conversation.

Ruth pointed me to Psalm 32 tonight, vs. 6. 'Let everyone who is godly pray to you... surely when the mighty waters rise they will not reach him. You are my hiding place; you will protect me from trouble and surround me with songs of deliverance.'

The scheduled appointment at the Cancer Centre for chemotherapy the next morning had to be postponed. A blood test revealed a low white cell count and so Ali was told she would be given medication to boost this. It would mean, though, it would be Thursday at the earliest before she could be given her next course of chemo. Ali was disappointed at this delay, initially, but she wrote that evening of how the postponement proved to be to her eventual blessing...

Monday 21ˢᵗ *(Still in the Hospice)*

Bishop Alan Abernethy visited the Hospice today. Paul knows of
him from his time in Ballyholme – he knows Heather and Steve. He
came in to see me. – they chatted about their connections in Bangor.
Heather is pregnant. Great news! He asked about my faith. I said it
was strengthened by this experience.

He said something like, "Are you writing all this down? You
should write down your experiences so you can encourage others by
your faith."

I had told him nothing about my spiritual journey, my hope of
encouraging others and definitely not that that I have a file on the
computer called 'my book'! He seemed to just know it by looking at me.

Caroline, the C. of I. chaplain, called it 'a God moment,' when we
talked about it later. Really encouraging – gives me hope for a future.

That evening, as Paul and Ali discussed their meeting with
Bishop Abernethy both commented happily, if indeed somewhat
incredulously, on how Ali had already started making notes for a
book and what an inspiration his remarks had been. They reckoned
he must have wondered at the knowing smile they had given each
other when he was dispensing such wise advice.

Husband and wife recognised the planning of God in the events
of that day, and together they thanked Him for the outcome of it.
"Just think," Ali enthused, "if I had been well enough to go for my
chemo I would not have been here when the Bishop called. And I
would hate to have missed that visit!"

They both agreed Caroline had been right. It had been a
uniquely uplifting experience for Ali. Undoubtedly 'a God moment.'

CHAPTER 16

I THANK GOD FOR HER

Although beset with a growing number of medical problems Ali never lost the thrill of being a mother, the devotion of being a daughter or the joy of being a wife. The strength of her family ties often kept her going through many of the most difficult days.

She cherished the times she was well enough to enjoy doing something simple with the boys when their dad brought them in. One such occasion was on Tuesday 22 April, and she recounted it that evening...

I slept most of the day. Paul brought the boys in during the after-noon. They watched DVD's and Mark and I did an atlas sticker book!

It sounded so ordinary when she described it but it was plainly very precious as she was experiencing it. She was too sore to be out of bed but Mark took his shoes off and climbed up beside his mum. With him tucked in at her side Ali, the mum, took great pleasure in helping her little boy stick the proper flags beside each country in his 'atlas sticker book.'

Her dad called regularly and on that Tuesday evening he and Christine took Ali out for a drive. They went the short distance to Belfast Castle and Ali so much appreciated the opportunity to have a short, if painful, walk 'in the fresh air.'

Ali's Aunt Margaret had already proved a great help to the Watson family during Ali's illness and her niece's diary entry the next day showed how grateful she was for the attention her aunt and her dad showed her...

Wednesday 23rd *(Hospice)*

...Auntie M called and brought her choccy squares. She's going to take the boys tomorrow...

Dad took me out for lunch – well he had lunch – I was fed here – had a scone and a cinnamon latte. Felt like a normal person and had very little pain so we went for a wee walk too. It was lovely to see him.

At least some of the discomfort Ali was experiencing was coming from severe bladder problems and the next day she was moved to the Cancer Centre where she was due to commence another round of chemotherapy and have a catheter fitted. She found later that day her pain was not quite so bad and she was so thankful to God for His provision of this relief. That night she wrote...

Thursday 24th   *(Hospice to Hospital)*

Realised later that God in His mercy has eased my pain. I told Him earlier I didn't know if I could cope with much more. He has eased my pain so I can deal with the catheter and the chemo. Couldn't have handled all 3. Must remember I can trust Him!

Pain eased before catheter went in

Paul came in tonight – he wasn't planning to but he wanted to and I needed him so much and was so relieved. He even brought pizza! Will probably be comatose tomorrow so no point in him coming in...

It was evident to all who came to visit Ali that her unshakeable trust in God was helping her cope with each and every distressing situation. The following day she was encouraged by a visit from

Ruth Potts, a family friend, who had been a counsellor in the Hospice and had then been diagnosed with cancer, and had subsequently undergone treatment herself. Ruth had personal experience of the disease from two very relevant angles and knew exactly how Ali felt, and what to say in the circumstances.

Paul had thought he wouldn't be in the next day, but with Ali having been through a treatment session he couldn't rest before seeing his very-ill wife. He arrived during the evening and while he was there Ali and he discussed a very practical issue. Should they employ someone to look after the housework to allow Paul to concentrate on the more personal concerns of their situation. This discussion led Ali to deeper, and more worrying long-term concerns for the days ahead. Her prime solace was again her total faith in her heavenly Father, and His will for her. After Paul left, much later, she expressed her thoughts on the matter, with obvious emotional unease but contrasting spiritual strength, in her journal...

Friday 25th

... Paul came in tonight – he brought me strawberries and clean clothes... all good! Hoping to start looking for a cleaner to free Paul up to look after the kids and me. He's coming round to the idea!

I'm coming round to the idea of being ill – actually ill to the point I can't do normal things for a while! It's hard – lots of tears and some guilt at not wanting to go home yet – too scared – still lots of things to sort out and keep remembering God is in control. He can heal me even where medicine fails. He will be with me. He will not let me drown...

Having returned to the Hospice following the spell of treatment in the Cancer Centre Ali had a visit from two church elders, her aunt Beenie and the ever-attentive Paul, all in the same day. The elders afforded her spiritual sustenance and the others the comfort of close companionship. There was also a different approach to pain relief. 'The new pain lolly thing,' she called it...

Friday 2nd May   *(Outside!)*

Paul came this morning. We just relaxed and watched a DVD.
Got a new painkiller – sort of rub it on the inside of your mouth...
Elders – David and Michael came and talked and prayed. Was
lovely to talk over some of the stuff I've been reading and thinking
about. I said my Isaiah quote was from the Living Bible – rivers of
difficulty – you will not drown. I don't have the version and Davey
offered me his – I persuaded him to keep it!
Beenie came in for a while. We chatted and tidied and laughed
as usual, and then she left as I needed to sleep. The new pain lolly
thing wasn't instant but I did get a really good sleep.
While I was sleeping Davey left in a new Bible for me – New
Living Translation – a lovely girly version too! Such a lovely present!

Amazingly I'm now sitting outside. Can't believe it – haven't left
my room much since I got back – just to have a bath I think! Weather
is mild and sun comes out now and then. Finally got a leg bag for my
catheter friend which really helps!

It was Bank Holiday weekend and although one day was pretty
much the same as any other for Ali it did mean that a number of
her friends and relatives were off work and free to visit – or babysit.
Peter and Niky had the boys away to Tollymore Forest Park in Co.
Down for the day and Paul and some others thought they would
like to take Ali out for a short break in the afternoon. It did not
turn out to be as enjoyable an excursion as they had all hoped it
would, however. Thinking back on that outing the following day,
when she had regained sufficient relief and composure to collect
her thoughts Ali wrote...

Tuesday 6th May

Was so good to see everyone yesterday, but disaster struck. You know how it is. You let optimism creep in and you think anything is possible. We – (me and Paul, J and A and Beenie) went to Belfast Castle – thought we'd have a wee wander, maybe coffee.

It was a beautiful day. The grounds were full of sunburnt people and there was a wedding at the Castle. We had a short slow wander but I was in agony after a few minutes...

Came back here and I was really upset. I cried so much I'm sure I was dehydrated. They gave me something to calm me and help me sleep. It didn't work! ...

Those were Ali's rather painful memories on a none-too-inspiring Bank Holiday but as she continued about the Tuesday, the day in which she was writing, her recollections were of something more rewarding. Interesting things had happened. Ali recorded another milestone in her acceptance of her condition and the tremendous spiritual boost she received from the visit of a friend...

...Today was better.

Morning frustrating but eventually got sorted. Talked to Dr. Alan – always lovely. Ken got me a wheelchair. Spark of inspiration I had this morning.

We headed to Abbeycentre. Wheelchair was great. I can do so much more when not irritating the catheter. We even had lunch at the noodle place in the food-court. Then went to M&S. Paul wheeled me rather than packing me into the car again!

Amazingly I had no bother with the chair – wasn't aware of people looking and managed to manoeuvre round the shops OK. Don't really care what people think – I'd rather be out than stuck in bed...

Slept solidly for 3 hours when we got back!

Nicola W came tonight – was so lovely to see her. She brought me a beautiful gift – the angel of courage.

More than that she says my illness and watching me deal with it and praying for me has brought her back to God. Nicola has been such a good friend since we met 'properly' at MOPs. I thank God for her...

Ali thanked God for Nicola, but it was Ali's attitude in her illness that had seen her friend 'brought back to God.'

Surely Nicola had good reason to thank God for her, too.

CHAPTER 17

THIS IS MIRACLE TERRITORY

On Friday 9th May a nurse was doing a routine temperature check and discovered that Ali's temperature had spiked alarmingly. Medical staff in the Hospice contacted her care team in the Cancer Centre and they advised she should 'come over' as soon as possible.

Paul was up at Ravenhill Rugby Ground watching an Ulster match but God had His plans in place for His suffering child. Two friends, Laura and Naomi called to see Ali but they ended up helping in her immediate need. They kept the conversation light-hearted as they talked Ali through the thought of another transition, while packing her stuff. Laura even helped her friend put on her shoes and socks. Having done all they could by way of preparation Laura and Naomi then drove Ali the few miles across Belfast to the Cancer Centre at the City Hospital. Ali had phoned Paul and by the time she arrived at her newest treatment location he was there to meet her.

The following day Ali recorded another thought-provoking spiritual outcome of Laura and Naomi's visit and involvement the previous evening. She reflected...

Saturday 10th May   (Cancer Centre)

... Laura lent me a book. 'Holiness in Hidden Places' by Joni Ericson Tada. I started reading it this morning. I've started to wonder what God's plan is – we're praying for healing and I'm getting worse! I read this today

'God will keep us. He'll help. He'll intervene. Perhaps just in the nick of time. Is that too close for comfort? Maybe. But our trust in Him was never meant to be comfortable – only close.
    And the nick of time is close enough...'

I don't know how bad God will let me get. I pray that He will heal me soon. But if He doesn't intervene until the nick of time, I pray I will have faith and hope and trust in Him as things get worse...

Later that day her dad called with Janet, Doug and little Iain. They had come across from Scotland to see her and Ali thought she was well enough to go out home with them for a few hours. This required a determined effort of mind and body to achieve, but it was worth it. She recalled another of those precious family get-together times in her journal next day...

Sunday 11th

Got home yesterday. J & D well and Iain lovely. All smiley and chirpy - sitting up on his own and loving to watch our boys.
    Our boys were in great form, excited to see us all. Paul had got them new toys at Niky's car-boot sale – a castle and an action man jeep thing.
    Euan wanted me straight in, saying "Come and see what I got mummy!"
    The boys are so adaptable...

The family had planned to repeat the exercise on Sunday but Ali wasn't up to it. After the good day on Saturday, Sunday and Monday were testing times. As she explained on Monday evening, that particular day had been one when physical weakness, emotional trauma and medical bad news all combined to leave her exhausted and apprehensive...

Monday 12ᵗʰ

I was supposed to go home yesterday for a barbeque but felt sick and stayed in hosp.

Today I feel like I've slept and cried all day. Dad brought J & D & I in on way to airport. I cried most of the time. I seem bed-bound today. Jan was going to help me wash but I did it myself – determined to force myself to do some things.

Told dad to tell God to do something because I can't cope any more. Can't go on like this.

Dad said this is a fallen world. It was not meant to be like this...

Doctor was in and he agrees with me that tumours are not decreasing. Going to stop chemo. Have also to decide on radiotherapy. It should reduce tumours but would also damage the skin.

When Paul came in that evening Ali told him of her earlier conversation with the doctor. Her husband was upset when he heard the medical team had decided to stop the chemotherapy. It seemed such a setback. The future ahead loomed up so uncertain.

What was there left? Were there any viable alternatives? Where, or to whom, could they look for hope?

His only resource was to turn to the ultimate refuge, a knowledge superior to medical science, the power behind the universe. "God has to do it now. This is miracle territory," he concluded.

The gradual realisation of the gravity of her condition presented Ali, the wife and mother, with a desperately difficult personal obstacle to overcome. She expressed this after a visit by two elders from her church fellowship on May 14, writing...

Gilbert and David were in. G. talked about recognising the sovereignty of God. I need to trust God – whatever the outcome. That means accepting the fact that I might die and handing my family over to God. I need to let everyone else fight for my healing while I

find rest in God.
    This is easier to write than do!

    I miss my boys. I feel like I'm not part of them anymore. Paul is potty training Euan – we were going to wait until I was well enough – but we can't now...

The prospect of having at some stage, whether sooner or later, to be separated from her two lovely little boys was breaking Ali's heart. The following day was one of intense emotional struggle. When it came to confining it to the pages of her journal, she noted...

Thursday 15th May

    ...Paul brought the boys in for lunch. We went out to the terrace – me in the w'chair, so they could run about. Mark kept saying "I love you." I kept crying! I cried too much when they were there – kept thinking I wasn't going to see them properly again. Very negative. Also aware of being selfish – thinking I've been cheated out of my life as a mum...

    Ruth Shaw came in tonight with a promise God gave her 9 years ago. He laid it on her heart to give it to me.
    Isaiah 54 v. 13
    All your sons will be taught by the Lord, and great will be your children's peace...

    God will teach my boys whether I live or die and I will see them in eternity...

    I'm starting to trust God more with my family. There is a big struggle between
    Trusting our sovereign God to look after us and our loved ones, whatever the outcome – His will be done, and

Praying – 'wrestling in prayer' for healing – almost trying to convince God – as Jesus did in the Garden of Gethsemane. Although He knew the outcome He asked God to take away His cup of suffering.

Matt. 26 v. 39
    Yet not my will but Yours be done.

That's it. Isn't it? I must want God's will although I make my request.
I must trust that His will, whatever that may be, will be best and that He will look after my loved ones.

Faith involves making a decision to trust God and placing my future in His hands. It's acceptance of not knowing, of not being certain of everything, but being absolutely confident in Him.

That had obviously been a landmark day in Ali's encounter with her emotions for next afternoon she recorded the result of her maternal and spiritual musings...

Friday 16th May

I have given things over to God
my husband
my boys
my future as a mum
I have repented of
my selfishness
my feeling of being cheated

God knows my heart. He knows how truly I have given things up. I am doing my best to release all.

Talked to Davey this morning about lots of things including some of the above. He says others are encouraged by our faith. To me it is the only option.

A few days later Ali needed to have a blood sample taken but the nurses had great difficulty finding a vein in her bruised arms. Her reaction to that unpleasant experience demonstrated how close she had become to God. She was learning to rest in Him, and to talk to Him, about everything. Her diary entry that evening illustrated that intimacy...

No matter how often we talk about prayer, how important it is, how God hears all etc. we still forget. Today I needed blood taken. They tried my right arm and it was too bruised, so tried right hand and really sore and no joy so said they would get a doctor. Eventually another nurse came and tried the other arm. I lay still trying not to think about it. She said she could feel a vein but it was very faint.

Suddenly I started praying, "Please God bring up that vein," over and over.

She said, "It's getting stronger but still deep."

I prayed, "Bring it to the surface. Please! Please!"

Eventually she got it and all the blood no problem!

It was like I was praying frantically and silently and she was giving me a commentary on the results of my prayer!

By June 1 Ali was finding the emotional strain and physical pain increasingly distressing. She poured out her heart on paper in two poignant journal observations that day...

I must keep on praying for healing. It's hard to get motivated. I cry a lot. Especially with dad.

I have said to God, "I'm ready for the outcome either way. Just please don't let me suffer anymore!"

CHAPTER 18

GOD ISN'T LETTING ME KNOW!

Sarah-Anne and Nicola were two of the many friends from Glenabbey who visited Ali during her illness and she always found the time they spent with each other uplifting. The three of them prayed and read the Bible together with one of their favourite readings, the one they either began with or ended up with, being Psalm 23.

In early June Sarah-Anne was touched to receive a text from Ali. She had obviously been contemplating her worsening situation and yet was resting in the promises of their special Psalm. All the treatments that could be tried had been tried and Ali summed up her feelings in the few poignant words, 'Maybe this is my green pastures.'

Her resolute and resigned faith in God, tempered occasionally by the very natural elements of uncertainty, became evident as she grew increasingly dependent on painkilling drugs with disease tightening its grip on her weakening body. Diary entries became less frequent as the emotional and physical struggle intensified, but one evening she wrote...

Monday 16th June

... I trust God to look after my family and that is the most important thing – Isaiah 54 v. 13
I am ready to go to be with God, I think.

Ali had now entered the domain of long and difficult days and often sleepless and seldom pain free nights with the struggle to retain sanity taking priority over systematic journal entries. But exactly a week later she recorded...

Monday 23rd June

Hebrews 10 v. 19
'And so we can boldly enter heaven's Most Holy Place because of the blood of Jesus... And since we have a great High Priest who rules over God's people, let us go right into the presence of God, with hearts fully trusting him...'

I still don't know if I will live or die. I am preparing to die but must remember either way I can approach God through Jesus our great High Priest.

The following day Ali had an encouraging visit with a recurring theme that never failed to cheer her often-fainting heart. She recalled it briefly in the afternoon...

Tuesday 24th June

Ruth Shaw came in this morn. She read John 10 reminding me I am a sheep with a Good Shepherd. Also read Psalm 23 – both saying the Good Shepherd is always with me and goes before me.

By mid-July the long stay in the Cancer Centre was beginning to get Ali down. The medical staff were most attentive and the care she was being given second to none, but still the sameness of everything, and no sign of anything even resembling an improvement in her condition led to her developing an irrepressible desire. There was a single goal she longed for more than anything else. She had spoken to Paul about it often, and identified it in one of her by-now rare journal jottings...

Monday 14th July

... I went home on Saturday and saw the boys. I just want to get home for good.

Some days can be very dark in here – I've been away now for over 3 months. I'm wasting away just lying in bed and I think I'm not capable of anything but if I could just get home I would have a purpose.

Sometimes all I can do is repeat over and over, 'the Lord is my shepherd I have all that I need,' until peace comes.

Ali had her wish granted on Monday 21 July. She was allowed to go home and thought it wonderful to be in her own house, and particularly her own bed, once more. Paul took charge of administering her medication and the boys made occasional trips upstairs to give their mum a hug. Family and friends came to visit and Ali was pleased to see everyone, but only for short periods.

The only downside was the awful, overpowering weakness. A couple of times when she made the ultimate effort to be 'normal' and come downstairs she was soon hankering to be back up in her room again.

On Wednesday evening Ali summarised her reaction to being at home, to having her utmost human wish fulfilled, in a brief diary entry...

Wed. 23rd July   *(Home)*

Got home on Monday afternoon. A bit overwhelming. Have no energy. Spending most of the day in bed. A District Nurse calls every day. They've been lovely and I have confidence in them.

My verse for today is Isaiah 54 v. 13

All your sons will be taught by the Lord, and great will be your children's peace.

Being at home was what Ali had wanted, but unfortunately on this occasion it was to be a temporary interlude rather than a permanent arrangement..

Late on Saturday evening Ali's temperature shot up alarmingly and she felt even more sick and sore than usual. Paul called the out-of-hours doctor and when he had seen her he concluded that she ought to be readmitted to the Cancer Centre.

The doctor made a few phone calls and just before midnight Ali was taken by ambulance back into the familiar surroundings of a single room in Ward 1. The nurses there knew her case from previous stays and attended to her at once, taking the necessary steps to make her comfortable.

One of the side effects of her illness and treatment was that Ali's left leg swelled up to the extent that she could barely walk. The provision of support stockings meant that she could leave the bed if ever she felt like it, and shuffle to the bathroom.

Again Ali yearned to be at home. She found it depressing to be so sick and weak in a place where all the patients on her floor were also extremely ill.

On the morning of Wednesday 6 August Ali was told that she was going to have her wish granted. Paul came to be with her until the ambulance arrived to transfer her, but what a long day that turned out to be. Recognising Ali's frustration, her husband enquired on a couple of occasions when the ambulance was due to come, only to be informed by equally frustrated staff that they had been told the ambulances were 'all busy' and 'one would be there later.

Each of them had something different to do while waiting, however. For Ali it was a taxing physical challenge to overcome. For Paul it was an emotional interview to attend.

Ali's discharge from hospital came with one condition attached. Aware that she was going out to a house with stairs the physiotherapists told Ali they would like to see her attempt to make it up some stairs before letting her home. Paul accompanied her down to the Physiotherapy Department and watched as his wife battled up two short flights of stairs. He knew, and the 'physios' knew, what an effort that represented on Ali's part, but she was determined nothing was going to hinder her getting home!

Ali's consultant, the lady who had been in charge of her treatment since she was first admitted to the Cancer Centre said she wanted to see Paul to discuss his wife's treatment at home. That was only part of the story, though. There was much more to it than that.

When the consultant had gone over the drugs Ali was to be given, and the care package she was planning to arrange with the District Nursing team, she made the telling statement, "We have not planned to review Alison again, Paul."

Recognising this as doctor-speak for, 'sadly there is nothing more we can do,' Paul came in with a question. "What is the prognosis here, doctor? How long have we got?" he didn't really want to know, but thought he really ought to know.

"We are talking in weeks rather than months," the consultant replied. "Alison is very ill. Are you prepared for this, Paul?"

"Yes, I think I am," was the distraught husband's response. "As prepared as I could ever be."

They were both in tears.

It was hard going back to Ali's bedside after that revelation in a consultation but Paul managed to do it and they settled down to wait once more.

The ambulance eventually arrived at 8 o'clock in the evening and Ali was returned to her beloved Greenisland home yet again.

Two days later, in one of her final journal entries, Ali, who must have been aware that recovery was now deep 'into miracle territory,' wrote...

Friday 8th August   *(Home again)*

We're still praying for healing, but really I'm concentrating on the day-to-day things – tiredness, bowels, aching legs, stinging wounds. I just want to be comfortable. Who knows how long I have got?
Only God – and He isn't letting me know!

CHAPTER 19

I'VE MADE IT!

The climbing-the-stairs test had proved and reinforced Ali's resolve. She was soon setting herself further goals.

When the ambulance crew brought her home that Wednesday evening they wanted to help her up the stairs.

"No," Ali insisted "I can make it myself."

And she did. It was a slow, and no doubt both painful and uncomfortable climb, but she made it, unaided. And now she was back into her own bedroom, and her own bed, the much hankered-after focus of her Cancer Centre dreams.

When she came to recognise herself, although never having been told it by anyone, that her life was now being measured in days, Paul encouraged Ali to identify two further targets they hoped were achievable. In course of conversation with her in the middle of one night when she couldn't sleep and he was too on-edge to sleep, he said, "I think we should aim for you seeing Euan's birthday and Mark starting school."

Euan's birthday was on August 16.

And Mark's first day at school was scheduled to be September 1.

Could she make it? Would God allow it?

There were times when Paul wondered if it would ever be possible.

Ali was totally confined to bed by that time. The boys popped in every now and then to tell her something they considered ever so important. Or there were times when it was just to give her a kiss and a hug then off they would go again.

Paul was up and down the stairs hundreds of times a day. When his wife was awake he had invariably something he wanted to ask her or say to her. And when she wasn't he stooped over her, just to check she was still breathing. It reminded him of happy days gone by, when Ali used to lean over the boys when they were asleep as tiny babies. Constantly, hauntingly ringing at the back of his mind was the distressing description of deterioration, with the possibility of suddenly fatal consequences, the singularly-upset signing-off oncologist had spelt out. And the pertinent, poignant, penetrating question, "Are you ready for this, Paul?"

By then carers were coming in four times a day to attend to Ali's medical and physical needs, and she didn't like this at first. The carers were gentle and understanding but their ministrations involved a certain loss of dignity which got to her. Her personal pride as a woman and a mother was totally shattered. Yet she had no alternative initially but to accept, and then gradually come to appreciate, their calls.

The Saturday of Euan's eagerly awaited third birthday came around with Ali still fit to enjoy it in as far as her rapidly-weakening bodily frame would allow.

Beenie had bought a birthday cake in the shape of a racing-car, and helped organise a party on the day. Lawson and Christine, Janet and Doug and Aunt Margaret joined her, Paul, Mark and 'the birthday boy' in a sad but significant marking of the occasion, downstairs. To call it a 'celebration' would have been a misnomer. No one really felt in party mood.

Before the birthday cake could be eaten, or even cut, someone had to light, then blow out, the three candles on it. This privilege ought to have been reserved for Euan, but on this occasion someone else very special just had to be involved. His mum.

Everyone climbed the stairs in a straggly line and piled into the bedroom. It was standing room only as Paul held up the cake and someone lit the candles. Then Ali leaned over as far as she could and placed an arm round Euan's shoulders. A voice said "One – two- three- go!" and mother and son blew mightily and out went the candles, leaving a trail of greyish-black smoke to curl up in the middle of the circle of faces.

The packed in people sang spontaneously, 'Happy birthday to Euan!' and clapped softly. Euan smiled broadly. And Ali cried silently.

It was now time for the loving family-friends to head back down to the living room. Ali encouraged them to, "Go down and let Euan play with his presents."

They heeded her instruction, leaving her to sink back gratefully into her pillows and thank God for permitting her the privilege of blowing out her little three-year-old's birthday candles.

One goal achieved. Only one more to go...

Deane Houston called regularly at the home to read the Bible and pray with Ali, always assuring her that she was 'constantly in the thoughts and prayers of everyone at Glenabbey.' The church pastoral worker was amazed at the depth of Ali's faith as they had deep spiritual discussions. These were sometimes centred on the reading Ali often requested, Psalm 23. They turned to this passage so often for its inescapable relevance to Ali's situation, touching as it did on issues like passing 'through the valley of the shadow of death' and dwelling 'in the house of the Lord forever.'

Paul and Ali were extremely grateful to God for Deane and their Christian friends in the church family who encouraged and supported them in so many practical ways through so many trying days.

The hands-on, in-house care demonstrated by Davy, an elder in the church, was a powerful example of this. He called at the door one evening and said, "Don't you worry about preparing anything to eat tomorrow evening, Paul. I will be round to make you an evening meal."

This was wonderful. Paul had recognised from church connections that Davy was 'a good cook,' but he had no idea just how good. And not having any idea what to expect he welcomed their friend the following afternoon, watched him deposit a selection of bags and boxes in the kitchen, and left him to it.

There was soon an appetising smell drifting out of the kitchen, and Paul, who was upstairs with Ali and the boys, wondered just what was going on down there. He was soon to know.

Just before he was ready to serve, Davy appeared up in the bedroom with a number of decorative candles. These he placed strategically among all the tell-tale signs of serious illness, and lit them. Having ensured that the ambience was to his liking he then proceeded to carry up, and serve, course by course, a three course meal to the family.

What Paul and Ali found particularly heart-warming about this entire home-cooked meal experience was Davy's choice of menu. He had remembered from past, and more relaxed, meals together with Paul and Ali that the now gravely-ill church member and friend loved ginger chicken. So ginger chicken was the meal on the menu for that evening!

Around that time the carers were beginning to have difficulty getting around Ali's bed to allow them to administer the more delicate level of care she required. They suggested to Paul that they would arrange for a hospital bed to be delivered to the house and thought this could be placed in one of the downstairs rooms for ease of access. Paul, though, had other ideas.

He wanted to minimise any disruption to the normal routine for Ali in her frail state, and so was determined if there was any way it could be accommodated in their bedroom that was where it would go. To make this possible, while still leaving the carers enough space to get on with their work, Paul did some experimental furniture moving. Eventually he came upon the best arrangement he could with the new bed beside their own bed, with sufficient space for movement around it. That meant that he would still be on hand to care for Ali both day and night which was what they both wanted.

When Ali was asked if she was happy with the new layout she replied, "I am. As long as I have a clock on the wall that's all I need."

As her condition continued to deteriorate further, watching the clock on the wall when alone could have been a depressing occupation for Ali. Time was ticking away. Minutes became hours and hours made days, and still she was growing weaker. Yet regardless of both her position and condition Ali kept her faith focused on God. When her mind was clear and her pain bearable she repeated her two consolatory verses to herself, over and over again.

"The Lord is my shepherd; I have all that I need," and "All your sons will be taught by the Lord, and great will be your children's peace."

Family members rallied round and helped Paul out where they could. His parents made frequent trips from Bangor to look after the boys and his mum was pleased to discover something very simple, but very practical, she could do to help.

By late August Paul realised that although he had Mark's new school uniform stored away for the next week he didn't have the name labels sewn on. Granny Watson was good with needle and thread and it was a labour of love for her to put her skill to good use and see Mark completely kitted-out in accordance with school regulations.

Every little helped in those days when Paul was so busy. There always seemed to be so much to think about. Am I really ready for this, whatever 'this' is? he was still asking himself often.

On Monday 1 September Paul had the boys up early. Mark was so excited to be putting on his new uniform for real. He had wanted to try it on so many times and he thought this day would never come! Just before they left for the short walk to Greenisland Primary School Paul took Mark up to the bedroom to let his mum see him all dressed up and ready to go.

What a special moment. Her little boy was about to become a schoolboy. And she had so much wanted to see this day.

Paul took a photo of him in his uniform beside his mum's bed. Ali was unbelievably weak but tried to sit up for the picture. Then it was time to set off for school.

Mark enjoyed the morning and one of the great things about that school day was it finished at lunch time. He had so many stories to tell his mum and dad when he arrived home, and also something special to show them.

His P1 teacher usually took a photo of each of her new pupils engaged in a play activity of some kind during their first week in class to keep as a record for herself, and to give to their parents. Having learnt of Ali's critical condition, however, she made a point of taking Mark's picture and sending it home with him that very first morning.

Paul collected him and as soon as they arrived into the house it was up to mum's room once more. Top priority for him was to let her see his photo.

It was a big struggle for Ali. Her eyesight was beginning to fail and she peered intently at the photo before saying with all the deep feeling of a proud mum, "That's lovely son!"

That photo was possibly the last thing Ali saw.

It had been touch and go but she had achieved her goals. She had been spared sufficient breath to blow out Euan's birthday candles and sufficient sight to see Mark's first school photo.

God had allowed it.

Ali summarised her feelings in a few words later that afternoon.

Although heavily sedated she said to Paul with a deep but satisfied sigh, "I've made it!"

CHAPTER 20

MUMMY'S NOT SICK ANYMORE

That Monday was the start of a dramatic week.

It was a week in which Paul found himself having to switch between, and manage, totally contrasting mind sets.

Mark was settling in well at school and as he picked him up each day dad listened as his little son described eagerly what the teacher, or the new friends he was making in class, had said or done that morning. Life was all so wonderful and fresh to him. Paul tried hard to focus on what he was being told so that he could respond appropriately, if not entirely enthusiastically.

That required a supreme effort, as his thoughts were usually taken up with what was going on at home.

Ali's condition was deteriorating rapidly.

The cancer had taken control of her body.

Her eyesight had gone and she was gradually losing the ability to speak.

Beenie moved in and this proved a blessing. She was able to use her nursing skill to help Paul attend to Ali, and her maternal experience to support him in caring for the boys.

Paul made 'smoothies' for Ali to drink. She had always loved them in her healthy days and now Paul reckoned they would be easy to swallow and yet provide some vital nourishment for a frail frame.

District nurses called periodically to dress Ali's wounds.

Family and friends were praying constantly, though not quite sure what to ask God for Ali. Was it restoration or release? Best, they thought, to ask that God's will be done and leave the outcome to Him. They knew Ali had already done this herself months ago.

On Thursday morning Paul was alone with Ali in the bedroom, just sitting beside her. She was gravely ill, unconscious, emaciated, and bore no resemblance whatsoever to the wonderful, witty, vibrant woman he had married nearly seven years before.

He was struggling with mixed emotions. That's not my Ali lying there, he thought. I hate seeing her like this. All I want is for her to be free from pain. To be released from this misery. To go to heaven, where she will be a perfect and pain-free person forever.

This line of reasoning was contradicted by a feeling of guilt. Am I right to be thinking like this? he wondered. How can I wish her away? How will I cope with looking after Mark and Euan without her around if, and more likely, when, she leaves us?

It was a dilemma, and as he was to learn later, one encountered by many Christian friends with loved ones terminally ill and overcome by utter physical weakness.

All he could think to do was to bow quietly and commit Ali, the boys and the future for all of them to God. It was the only answer, the sole source of any kind of peace.

Deane came to visit about 10 o'clock that evening. He and Paul were sitting in the bedroom speaking to one another in hushed tones when Ali began to move her arms jerkily, as if trying to communicate in some way.

"Do you want a hug?" Paul whispered, rising from where he had been sitting on the end of the bed and moving round beside her. He then lifted Ali's arms and gently placed one of her hands on each of his strong shoulders. To complete the pattern Paul proceeded to set his own hands on his wife's now-bony shoulders, and gaze down at her face. Beenie, who had always been conscious of presenting Ali's personal appearance as her niece herself would have wanted, whatever the circumstances of her illness, had already combed her red hair, leaving it spread out neatly, and contrasting starkly with the white of the pillow.

"Just stay there like that for a minute while I read to you both," Deane said softly.

Opening his Bible he began to read the passage which had so

often been Ali's comfort, and one of their dominant themes for spiritual discussion, when she was still well enough to appreciate or discuss anything. This time though it was to be Psalm 23, the personalised version. Paul listened, and he trusted Ali heard, as Deane read...

'The Lord is Ali's shepherd, Ali shall not be in want.

He makes Ali lie down in green pastures, he leads Ali beside quiet waters, he restores Ali's soul.

He guides Ali in paths of righteousness for his name's sake.

Even though Ali walks through the valley of the shadow of death, Ali will fear no evil for you are with Ali; your rod and your staff, they comfort Ali.

You prepare a table for Ali in the presence of Ali's enemies,

You anoint Ali's head with oil; Ali's cup overflows.

Surely goodness and love will follow Ali all the days of Ali's life, and Ali will dwell in the house of the Lord for ever.'

A heavenly peace descended on the room when Deane finished his reading. He and Paul were conscious of the reality of a divine presence. This was a real 'God moment.' Had Ali's personal, much-talked-about, often-prayed-to shepherd come to guide her through the maze of dark, steep, rough and obstacle-strewn paths that crossed 'the valley of the shadow of death?'

That was what it felt like.

Deane prayed before leaving for home and Paul settled down in the darkened room to take the 'first shift' by his wife's bedside. Beenie had earlier slipped in to say 'Goodnight' to Ali and tell Paul that the boys were both sound asleep and she would go to bed for a few hours and they would change over 'between three and four' to allow him 'to get some sleep before the morning.'

That arrangement was not to prove necessary...

Paul sat watching Ali in her deep sleep. The only sound to stir the silence was her faint breathing.

Then it stopped. It took Paul a moment to recognise what had happened. Ali's breathing had ceased. She was gone. She had departed for heaven. She had left to take up residence 'in the house of the Lord for ever.' Softly in her sleep.

The room was engulfed by a strange, utter stillness. There was a sense of total tranquillity.

It was pain-free peace and welcome release for Ali at last.

But what of Paul? He felt suddenly alone.

Nothing could have prepared him for the forlorn feeling of that moment. He hadn't been 'ready for this,' no matter how often he had tried to imagine it.

This was something completely different.

Yet he had to act. There was much to be done.

He rose, kissed the still figure in the bed on the forehead, and then knocked gently on the door of the next bedroom to waken Beenie. She hadn't been sleeping soundly and was immediately out on the landing.

"I think Ali has gone," Paul whispered. Beenie didn't need him to say anything. His shocked expression had conveyed the message as adequately as any words could have done.

When Beenie accompanied Paul into the bedroom and felt for Ali's pulse she confirmed what Paul was sure he already knew.

Yes. It was true. The person whose zest for life and approach to death they had both loved had succumbed. Ali had passed away.

Both then began to organise the difficult aftermath of the event.

Beenie agreed to go downstairs and get on the telephone. Her immediate priorities were to contact the out-of-hours doctor and a funeral director. Paul allowed her to get on with it, for before he could allow himself to be involved in organisational concerns there was a final family matter he wanted to address. And he had to do it soon.

Tip-toeing into Mark's bedroom Paul touched him on the shoulder, thus rousing him slowly. When the sleeping four year-old stirred himself awake in response to the gentle pressure from his dad's hand, Paul whispered to him, "Do you remember, Mark, how mummy talked about God having a job for her to do in heaven some day?"

"Yes," his son replied, sleepily.

"Well, God needs her to go and do that now. Would you like to say 'Goodbye' to her before she leaves?"

"Yes," Mark replied for the second time, more with-it now, and sliding out of bed.

With that Paul led him into the next room where his mum's body lay still and peaceful in the bed. Spontaneously, and as he had done so often before in life when she could respond, Mark leaned over and kissed and hugged the still-warm form of his mum when she couldn't.

"Goodnight, mummy," he said.

Then taking his dad's hand he went back into his own bed. Paul, who was fighting manfully to hold back the tears, wrapped the covers round him and bent down to kiss him.

"Night-night, Sparky," he said.

The next few hours were busy. The doctor came and went. The funeral director came and went. There were phone calls to be made to the next of kin, most of whom had been expecting the news they were to receive. They were happy for Ali, whose pain was over but sad for themselves and especially for Paul and the boys, as all of their pain of loss and separation was just beginning.

The night was almost over before Paul dropped exhausted into the bed Ali and he had bought, and loved, alone. The hospital bed stood beside it, forlorn and empty. Paul had asked the funeral director to make sure it was like that before the boys were ready to rise in the morning.

Before switching off the bedside lamp he spied something.

There, sitting on the little table beside the lamp was a notebook with a blue fabric cover which had a white flower surrounded by pale green leaves painted on it. It was tied in a neat bow with a maroon ribbon. Ali had made it at MOP's at least a year before.

It was her precious, personal journal.

Reaching across with a pang of conscience Paul picked it up.

He felt almost guilty. It was like trespassing into the realm of the confidential and intimate. Like callously disregarding a sign which said, 'Private Property. No Admittance.' He had never felt inclined to open it before.

Yet if he didn't feel free to read it now when would he?

Half-sitting up in bed he carefully untied the bow, let it fall open in front of him and began to read. He was immediately transfixed and transported back in time. It was gripping stuff. Then he turned back to the first page and went through the journal of his wife's jottings and soon the tears were flowing unchecked down his cheeks.

'*God is glorified by how you act in the fire,*' he read.

'*I cried so much I'm sure I was dehydrated,*' Ali had said.

'*Told dad to tell God to do something for I can't cope anymore,*' he read.

'*God will teach my boys whether I live or die and I will see them in eternity,*' Ali had said...

The memories came flooding back. Page by poignant page they hit him.

Here was another in-depth insight into what for many was a well-known fact.

His wonderful wife had been an outstanding woman of faith.

Having leafed through the journal a number of times Paul put his finger into the page dated Monday 21 April and held it there. It contained the recorded quote from Bishop Abernethy.

Ali had written '*He said something like, "Are you writing all this down? You should write down your experiences so you can encourage others by your faith.*'

Before eventually allowing his finger to slide out from that page and replacing the journal reverently on the bedside table where it had sat for months, Paul made a personal resolve. He would find some way of using what Ali had written down 'to encourage others' by her faith.

Paul had a very short time in bed before it was time to get up and attend to the mounting list of things to be done. His brother Peter was one of the first of the family members to arrive and offer his help and Paul had something to do where his companionship proved most welcome.

Despite all that had happened in the past few days, and all that was due to happen in the coming few days, Paul was determined to keep the routine of life as near normal as possible for the two boys. And this involved allowing Mark to complete his first week at school uninterrupted. Peter volunteered to accompany his grieving brother on the short walk there and back.

It was a crisp early September morning. There was a hint of approaching autumn in the clear air as Mark, dad and uncle Peter left the house. They had only gone a short distance when they were joined by two of Mark's friends who were also neighbours and who usually walked to school with him and his dad.

The three boys were chatting away when Mark remarked to his companions ever so matter-of-factly, "My mummy's not sick anymore."

The two friends didn't respond immediately for they weren't exactly sure what he meant. They knew Mark's mummy had been very ill for they had heard their parents talking about it, and what was more they hadn't seen her out and about for ages.

Peter and Paul were interested listeners, wondering where this declaration would lead to in conversation.

There was a short pause before one of the boys decided to express the bafflement of both. "What do you mean your mummy's not sick anymore?" he enquired.

Mark looked across at them with a look of mild exasperation. Imagine walking to school with boys who didn't even know an easy thing like that.

He then proceeded to explain what for the family and friends preparing to gather back at the house was an emotionally complex issue, in concise and very simple terms.

"Mummy has gone to heaven," he told them. "God has a job for her to do."

CHAPTER 21
THAT WAS AMAZING!

It was true. Mummy wasn't sick anymore.

It was true, too, that she had gone to heaven.

And it was also a tremendous consolation that her pain was gone and her eternity of joy had already begun.

For those who loved her and were left behind, however, there was a difficult period ahead. Although they were to prove extremely trying emotionally, the pain and loneliness of the days immediately following Ali's passing were considerably lessened by two factors.

The first of these was the visits from the stream of kind and caring friends who called to express their condolences and the other the seemingly endless list of things to be done.

In addition to the above there was, for Paul, a third and personal source of solace. That was the occasional dip into Ali's diary. When the pain of parting hit him in the rare, and often unexpected, quiet moments he was afforded during the day, and during wakeful moments in restless nights he would resort to what had already become for him a handwritten treasure. The young widower would read a little, weep a lot, and then be so thankful for the love he had been privileged to share with Ali, and so admiring of the exemplary faith she had displayed in God.

Tuesday 9 September was to be the day of the three services.

First of these was a family gathering in Lawson's house. To avoid undue stress for the boys Paul had agreed to Ali's dad's suggestion that he keep the coffin, and entertain many of the mourners, at his home. Thus it was there that family members met mid-morning to meditate on, and share, personal and precious memories of their cherished loved one, and praise God for the spiritual inspiration she had been to them all.

Then it was on from Greenisland to Roselawn Crematorium for a short but very touching committal. Gilbert Lennox, who had shared many spiritual experiences with Ali during her illness, and was the teaching elder from the Church, conducted this service, which was attended by both Paul and Ali's immediate families.

This was the devastating bit for them all. There was such a sense of finality about it.

Meanwhile back at Glenabbey people were gathering in subdued fashion and in huge numbers for a Thanksgiving Service for Ali's life. This was due to begin at 2'oclock but long before the scheduled start time the building was full.

Paul and the other family members were among the last to arrive and be ushered up to the seats reserved for them in the front rows. As he walked up to take his place Paul was dumbfounded. He was astounded at the sheer volume of people. Among them he caught a glimpse of a row of guys from his office in Lisburn Road Police Station.

The grieving husband and father was touched that they had made the effort to be there to help him celebrate the life and mourn the loss of his beloved Ali. Yet they were just a tiny percentage of this capacity congregation.

Who were all these others? They were from many walks of life, from many parts of the United Kingdom, from many churches and of all ages.

It was staggering.

And as the service began, then proceeded, the feeling of finality that had hit him at Roselawn was dispelled in Glenabbey. It was replaced by a sense of peace, engendered by the comfort of being surrounded by a multitude of caring friends in an atmosphere already charged with divine love.

The song, 'I Belong' was being played on CD as Paul and his group took their seats. The impact of the words, a modern presentation of the New Testament affirmation that 'nothing can separate us from the love of Christ,' helped fine tune his mind to the correct spiritual channel for the service to come.

With barely a spare seat left in the building David Mairs who had visited Ali so often in home, hospital and hospice rose to welcome the guests, express condolences to the family and give a brief outline of the proposed order of service.

Words didn't come easily, though. Tears would have. He was suddenly choked up with emotion.

David hadn't been looking forward to this. He had been invited to lead a thanksgiving service for the life of someone he had come to look upon as more than merely another member of the roll of Glenabbey. This was a close friend and, as he had discovered over the previous two years, a woman characterised by a remarkably practical and hands-on spirituality. She had lived her Christianity like she talked it.

When he came to pay tribute to Ali a short time later David referred often to Ali's journal. Paul had shown it to him and he was totally overcome by it. The entries, to him, provided a complete and accurate encapsulation of the life of the young woman. Her Christian faith, her love for and concern about her husband and boys, her gradual acceptance that God may be going to effect her healing in heaven rather than on earth. It was all in there.

Early in his tribute he told of how he had been, and many present could nod in agreement for they had also been, revitalised by going to visit her. He said, "Typical of Alison when you would go to visit her the first thing she'd ask would be, "And how are you doing? How's Viv? And how's your family? What's happening at the church?" I thought I was going to encourage her and share with her but often she was wanting to share with me what God was saying to her. It was a wonderful privilege."

Later he referred to a particular day when Ali had shared with him a few of the deep mental and spiritual struggles she was coping with almost on a daily basis. Davy quoted from her journal entry, adding his own reflections on the event.

"The following day she writes and I remember it well," he said.

'I have given things over to God. My husband, my boys, my future as a mum.

I have repented of my selfishness, my feelings of being cheated.

God knows my heart – he knows how truly I have given things up. I am doing my best to release all.

Talked to Davy this morning about lots of things including some of the above. He says others are encouraged by my faith. To me it is the only option.'

"This was Alison. So often she would say, "I don't have a choice. I have to deal with what comes my way. And so we spent many times focusing on the now. I never left without asking, "What will we pray for today?" And so she faced life one day at a time."

Preparing to bring his tribute to a close David made reference to Ali's love of Psalm 23. Quoting from another and one of her final insightful observations, he told the sympathetic congregation, "As her illness progressed Alison was not able to write as much as she would like. However, one of her last comments in the middle of July is,

'Sometimes all I can do is repeat over- The Lord is my shepherd I have all that I need, until peace comes.'

"And so on Friday 5th September at 00:50 peace came. Everything was ready and God took Alison to be with him forever.

And we are left inspired by her life and witness, encouraged by her faith in the midst of the fire, strengthened by her perseverance, humbled by her love for God and trust in her Good Shepherd. The Lord is Alison's Shepherd."

The softness, warmth and poignant personal references of Davy's tribute touched the hearts of the huge crowd. Many individuals were moved to tears by it.

Others were moved, not to tears but to praise and worship by the impact of the musical items at that service. The songs had been carefully chosen to reflect Ali's faith in God and assurance of His preparation for her future.

The church worship team led by Suzanne and Alistair Bennett provided the music as everyone sang 'Higher Throne' with the verse...

'And there we'll find our home; our life before the throne.
We'll honour Him in perfect song where we belong.
He'll wipe each tear stained eye as thirst and hunger die.
The Lamb becomes our shepherd king; we'll reign with Him...'

helping them focus on their friend's new state, position and condition.

No one present could have mistaken the continued emphasis on Psalm 23 as a constant comfort to Ali in her difficult days of illness as Deane Houston recounted the events of the evening of Thursday 4 September when he called round at the Watson home. It was to be the last time he was to see the one he had come to love and respect over the many occasions when they had shared spiritual thoughts and experiences together, alive.

He described the cup of tea in the kitchen with Beenie, the scene in the bedroom when Paul sat face to face with his wife with hands on each other shoulders, and what he had read. Then Deane proceeded to read the lovely shepherd Psalm, just as he had done that memorable evening.

He was visibly moved as he began with the promise of provision,

'The Lord is Ali's shepherd, Ali shall not be in want...'

Continuing on through to the promise of a protecting presence,

'Even though Ali walks through the valley of the shadow of death, Ali will fear no evil, for you are with Ali...'

And reading on down the Psalm to conclude with the promise of a heavenly destination,

'Surely goodness and love will follow Ali all the days of Ali's life, and Ali will dwell in the house of the Lord for ever.'

When Sarah-Anne Wilmont, one of Ali's close friends and someone who visited her often and appeared in occasional diary entries, was invited to sing a solo at the Thanksgiving Service choosing a piece was not a problem.

It just had to be the modern version of 'The Lord's My Shepherd.'

How often they had shared the thought of green pastures, endless mercy and an eternal home together. Now Sarah-Anne felt honoured to sing in memory of her friend and to the praise of God...

'The Lord's my Shepherd, I'll not want
He makes me lie in pastures green
He leads me by the still, still waters
His goodness will lead me home

And I will trust in you alone
And I will trust in you alone
For your endless mercy follows me
Your goodness will lead me home...'

Gilbert Lennox, when he stood up to address his second and infinitely larger audience of the day, began by remarking something everyone in the audience already knew.

"There was something different, something special, about this person," he declared. "What we would like to do now for a short time is explain the reason for that difference."

He then read from the Bible in 1 Peter chapter 1 verses 3 – 9.

Basing his talk on the Scripture reading, he commenced by pointing out that Peter was writing about 'new birth into a living hope through the resurrection of Jesus Christ from the dead.'

"Peter," he said, "was a witness of the resurrection of Jesus from the dead. He knew that the grave was not the end. That is the basis for the 'living hope' he writes about, and that is what makes Christianity different. We have a 'living hope' and 'an inheritance that can never perish, spoil or fade.'

This was real to Alison. She understood it. She believed it. And she found joy and strength in it through her faith...

Yet she had her questions. Some unanswered questions.

Alison never tried to hide this. She saw the fire was coming, and referred to this in her journal. What was God's plan in all of this?

Peter tells us. He writes about the possibility of having 'to suffer grief in all kinds of trials for a little while.' And he gives the reason. 'These have come so that your faith – of greater worth than gold, which perishes even though refined by fire – may be proved genuine and may result in praise, glory and honour when Jesus Christ is revealed.'

The trial was not to destroy faith, but to bring it out in all its glory. And Alison is a tremendous example of this. Despite all she went through, a shining faith and a stronger faith emerged.

Was it all worthwhile? We can only look at these things from the perspective of this life, but we cannot see them as Alison is privileged to see them now. We are seeing a vague image in black and white. She is looking at it in glorious technicolour.

For her the school bell has rung. Graduation has come. She has completed her course.

I would love to be a fly on the wall of heaven as God gives her the divine explanation of the plan of her life.

We read that our trials would 'result in praise glory and honour when Jesus Christ is revealed.' Alison knows all about that praise glory and honour now, for Jesus Christ has been revealed to her. She has seen him, and been welcomed by him in all His heavenly glory...

Alison's God is now speaking to us this afternoon through her. Each of us must ask ourselves are we prepared to face the future like she was. Do we have 'a living hope'?"

Having completed this stirring and challenging testimony to a remarkable life of faith and fortitude Gilbert announced the singing of another hymn, 'In Christ Alone.'

The final verse of that piece seemed so appropriate to the occasion, with many in the congregation reflecting on what they had already heard, and on the relevance of the words as they sang...

'No guilt in life, no fear in death;
This is the power of Christ in me
From life's first cry to final breath;
Jesus commands my destiny

No power of hell, no scheme of man:
Can ever pluck me from His hand;
Till he returns or calls me home
Here in the power of Christ I'll stand'

Before concluding the Thanksgiving Service in prayer the speaker had 'a couple of announcements' to make. One of these was to say that 'everyone would be very welcome to stay for tea, which had been provided in the house across the way.' The other was to intimate that 'Lawson would be available to speak to friends in the foyer after the service.'

Lawson had been Ali's dad, but what of Paul, Ali's husband?

He had something else on his mind.

When he came to the foyer he was aiming to walk on out through it to the car park. It wasn't that he didn't want to hang around and speak to the people filing out behind him. It was just that there were two special people he had to find.

Mark and Euan.

They had been picked up from school and brought to the church and Paul wanted to see them. In spite of his best efforts to make a bee-line for his boys he was waylaid by some friends who wanted to sympathise with him.

By the time he reached his two young sons he discovered that Uncle Peter had got to them first. They loved Peter, and they also loved what he was allowing, Paul suspected even encouraging, them to do.

That was splashing in the puddles.

They looked so happy. It came as a relief to their dad to see them so light-hearted, so carefree. Hundreds had been told in the service that their mum was now happy in heaven, and her boys now appeared so happy on earth. Could he be happy, though?

If he were to take on board the comments of the many people who sought him out in the car park and during the 'tea in the house across the way,' he ought to be.

Many in the course of their condolences said how the service had been 'such a fitting tribute' to such a lovely Christian woman, with some going on to add that 'it was just as she would have wanted it had she been planning it herself.'

Perhaps one of the most memorable quotes of that late afternoon as people were beginning to leave in twos and threes to find their cars, came from one of his police colleagues. The group of guys from Lisburn Road Police Station came across to him and one of them said both enthusiastically and sincerely, "Wow, Paul. That was amazing!"

It had been a tremendously up-and-down kind of a day for Ali's husband, family and friends.

Heart-rending yet heart-warming.

Endlessly active and emotionally draining.

God-honouring and honestly great.

And yes. What the man had said was true too. It was a simple and succinct way of summing it all up.

Absolutely amazing.

CHAPTER 22

THANKS, GUYS!

There was a flurry of activity for a few days following the Thanksgiving Service. Paul wanted to make sure he thanked all who had helped on that 'amazing' day with its strange blend of joy and gladness, grief and sadness. He told them that although he had felt an awful inner loneliness at the loss of his Ali, yet thanks to them he had also felt surrounded, and carried along by, a tangible sense of tremendous love. Some of the relatives and friends who had travelled to be present were still around and their company helped delay the descent into reality as well.

And no matter who came or went, or what else had to be done, the boys remained Paul's priority. He made sure Mark continued to go to school and Euan to playgroup each day..

By the end of the week the scene had changed on two of those three considerations.

Gradually and systematically Paul worked down the list of people to be thanked through texts and telephone calls. Gradually, too, and with sad partings, all the friends and relatives left for home to return to their jobs and generally get on with their lives.

Life for Paul was then beset by a sense of emptiness, of being on his own, with nothing to arrange or attend, plan for or supervise.

The previous nine months had passed in a constant round of hustle and bustle. In the early stages of Ali's illness there had been hospital appointments to go to, hospice visits to fit in, and babysitters to arrange.

Yet in spite of all the coming and going he made sure he always allowed time to talk to Ali, and God.

When Ali came home from hospital for good in August, life became even busier. There were the carers, members of the family and friends from church calling. Hardly ever a day passed but he had about a dozen different people dropping in at some stage and for a different reason. Paul was delighted to see all who came and invariably had some interaction with them. Then on top of all of that he had volunteered to take charge of giving Ali her medication under the supervision of Sue, the hospice-at-home nurse.

Regardless of how full his daily schedule became, however, there were occasional treasured moments when he had time to spend in the room with Ali, talking, listening, or sitting in the silence of shared love. And even later when her condition had deteriorated to the extent that she found coherent communication impossible she was still there. Still alive. Still a presence. Still his wife.

Now she was gone. Everything said about her in the Thanksgiving Service had been true. Loving wife and mother, devoted daughter, caring sister and sister-in-law, diligent and loyal church member, tremendous Christian, shining example, inspirational witness... Not a single tribute had been overstated.

Yet that was in the past. All the kind and sincere tributes were consoling to reflect on but they didn't fill the void. They could comfort his heart but they couldn't give him his wife back. Not that he would have wanted her back to pain and suffering, but how he just longed to be able to talk to her again, There were times when he thought, especially when the boys said something cute, 'I must tell Ali that,' and then it hit him ever so hard.

'I can't you know.'

During those early days of coming to terms with his new status as widower, Paul played one song a lot. Any time he found himself in the house alone, a situation which was happening more frequently, he felt drawn to switch it on. It was the song he had asked to be played as the congregation were assembling for the service on Tuesday, 'I Belong.'

He found the words, and the concept, consoling.
The chorus was particularly reassuring...

Nothing can take me from your great love
Forever this truth remains,
I belong, I belong to you,
I belong, I belong to you.

One evening he was in the kitchen. The boys were in bed and the song was playing. Paul was overcome by a sudden wave of anguish. Everything seemed to come in on him at once. The days of Ali's illness, the peace of her passing, the inspiration of her life, the impact of her journal, their love for one another and the everlasting love of God which had bonded them together all flooded over him in one irresistible torrent of grief and gratitude.

He stood with his back to a kitchen cupboard and cried. Then he allowed his back to slide down the door until he ended up sitting on the floor, still weeping.

Paul remained in that position for some time letting his emotions take over the moment. It seemed that the bottom had fallen out of his world.

Then another thought began to dispel the abject despair. Whether it was a sound from upstairs that triggered it, or the sight of a schoolbag on the floor he couldn't quite be sure, but slowly he didn't feel sorry for himself anymore.

Realising that he still had a very responsible duty to perform, a very urgent matter to address, he rose from the floor. 'I have to pull myself together here,' he determined.

'I still have the boys. These two boys are all I have now. My job is to be both mother and father to them. I will bring them up as their mum and I had often resolved we would. I will endeavour to teach them to be well-mannered, well-disciplined children with a respect for God and other people.'

For the last few years Paul had been so happy to have Ali and the boys and the promise of the presence of God. Now that Ali had changed positions and had gone into the immediate presence of God, he still had the boys and the unchanging promise of the presence of God. He reckoned he could work with that, for all of their sakes.

On the first Sunday after the Thanksgiving Service Paul decided to return to Glenabbey Church. He knew he would be among sympathetic friends there and he wanted to be present to worship God with all the fullness of his breaking heart.

He went with Brian and Andrea Duff. Brian and Andrea were one of the couples who had been close friends of Paul and Ali ever since they had joined the church at Glenabbey, and it was their holiday home in Portrush they had been in at Easter. It was hard going back, for the last time he had been in the building was at the Thanksgiving Service but the genuine warmth of the welcome he was afforded by all who saw him come in helped ease him through the return experience.

Paul thought he was coping reasonably well emotionally until it came the turn of the worship team to lead the congregation in praise. Everyone was standing singing heartily but when they announced, then began, 'In Christ Alone,' Paul broke.

The enthusiastic praise reminded him graphically of five days earlier when the capacity crowd had sung with such feeling...

In Christ alone my heart is found
He is my light, my strength, my song.
This Cornerstone, this solid ground
Firm through the fiercest drought and storm
What heights of love, what depths of peace
When fears are stilled, when strivings cease
My Comforter, my All in All
Here in the love of Christ I stand....

The words of the song, in addition to its connections and connotations, got him right in the heart. 'The heights of love' and 'the love of Christ' were what he had been hearing about dozens of times over during the previous days in 'I Belong.' Add to that fierce storms, stilled fears and ceased strivings and you had a recipe for bringing a tear to the eye of any recently-bereaved young Christian father.

Paul began to sob and his shoulders began to shake. Sensing how moved he was Andrea took a short sidestep and slipped her arm around him. When she saw this happen, Ina Slane who was standing directly behind him placed her hand gently on his shoulder and left it there.

Although overcome with grief Paul was tremendously comforted to feel the tender touch of genuine Christian friends. He knew instinctively that these people really cared for him deep down and that was a marvellous help.

Before the song was finished Paul felt all the inner turmoil cease, the sense of loneliness depart, and the seeds of a new confidence begin to sprout. It was as though the 'peace of God which surpasses all understanding' had arrived to 'take possession of his mind through Christ Jesus.'

Realising the part his friends had played in bringing about this transformation he turned to speak to them as they were settling into their seats again after the worship session.

"Thanks, guys!" he said softly, just loud enough for both of them to hear.

Little did he know but he hadn't needed to say anything. The smile on his lips and the glow on his tear-stained cheeks was all the thanks they needed.

CHAPTER 23

TEAM WATSON

Paul, the rugby player and fan, has always known, and been a strong advocate of the benefits of teamwork, not only on the pitch but also in every other aspect of life. Thus when faced with the responsibility and privilege of raising his two young sons that was how he approached it.

For the past two years it has been 'Team Watson'.

The idea is that all three team members play the game of life understanding each other's field position, looking out for each other and passing to each other, with all accepting that dad, who is the most experienced player, is captain. This allows him to make final decisions on overall game plans.

Paul had now much more time to spend with the boys and to devote to their needs and interests. He had been looking after them admirably for the last six months but in those days Ali, although ill, was always available. On difficult or delicate matters he could resort to the safety net of her opinion.

Questions beginning, "What do you think we should do about..?" usually initiated discussions leading to joint decisions.

Now he was left to make up his own mind on things. He was constantly asking God for guidance in prayer and telling the boys, the other team members, he was doing so.

When all necessary matters had been attended to following Ali's passing, Paul felt ready to return to work in November. This was only possible because of the support he received from members of his close family in caring for the boys and helping in the house. His mum and dad, Lawson and Christine and Aunt Margaret became chief babysitters. His mum also stepped into the role of housekeeper with his dad volunteering to help him look after the garden.

During the months he was off work Paul was contacted from time to time by his colleagues. Initially it was to enquire about Ali and then he had been so pleased to see them at the Thanksgiving Service. In the weeks following that they had been telling him they would be glad to see him back on duty with them, when he felt up to it.

They proved as good as their word, too.

When Paul returned to his duties in Lisburn Road Police Station he just slipped back into the routine, and was welcomed by his fellow-officers who were sympathetic and supportive.

As months passed Paul became convinced that he ought to embark on two separate projects in memory of Ali, to highlight her outstanding faith in God, and help others who were experiencing the challenges of cancer. The first of these was to have a story written incorporating excerpts from her journal, confident that this would, as Bishop Abernethy suggested, 'encourage others in their faith.' Secondly, he became keen to engage in some kind of fund-raising exercise for the Northern Ireland Hospice. Ali was afforded such first class care during her various stays there and Paul had come to appreciate the level of dedication displayed and care delivered by the staff so much he was determined to maintain his ties with them, helping practically if possible.

You are now holding the fulfilment of his initial ambition, and the other has also seen a diversity of activity on three separate occasions to date, each with very rewarding results.

On May Bank Holiday 2009 Paul organised a sponsored relay team to run in the Belfast City Marathon. It was a mixed group all of whom had known Ali from Glenabbey and were keen to do something challenging in her memory.

Paul had special T-shirts printed for the occasion. Each member of the team set out to complete his or her leg of the relay proudly wearing it. The shirts had the Northern Ireland Hospice logo on the front and a picture of Ali and the apt team name, 'Ali's Allsorts' emblazoned across the back.

This venture caught the imagination of many who learnt of it and the runners raised £5,000 for the Hospice through the generosity of their sponsors.

Although Paul kept in contact with the Northern Ireland Hospice and its fundraising team his next public involvement with them was not a fundraiser. He counted it an honour to be invited by the management to bring Team Watson along to switch on the lights on their outdoor Christmas tree in December 2009.

It was a magical evening.

Mark and Euan pushed the button and suddenly the tree, which had looked so drab in its dull dark-green, was brilliant and bright with light!

As everyone stood around it, with some remarking on its decoration and illumination and others coming across to thank the boys for 'the great job' done, something else, something unexpected, happened.

It started to snow!

A few light flakes came drifting down at first, almost unnoticed. Then they became larger and heavier.

The boys were mesmerised.

It was so wonderful. Just like the picture straight off a Christmas card. The dark and chill of a winter evening, the coat-clad crowd around the light-bright tree, and now to crown it all, the snow!

Mark and Euan were so excited to have switched on the lights on the tree, and not only that, as far as they were concerned they had switched on the snow as well!

With the winter past Paul embarked on organising his next fundraising endeavour for the Hospice. This one, though, was not for the faint-hearted, but for the fit and fearless.

He and a few of his friends arranged to abseil down the front of the Europa Hotel in Belfast city centre and this exploit raised a further £2,500 for the Northern Ireland Hospice.

This involvement with the much-appreciated charitable organisation helps Paul cope with the loss of his wife, knowing that the pain and suffering of others is being alleviated, just as Ali' s was, through their kindness and care.

This is not his only source of strength, however. He is encouraged in so many other ways as well. These range from the support of his family and the consideration of his colleagues to the spiritual refreshment and renewal he experiences from the services in Glenabbey and the contact with the many Christian friends he has made there. Some of these were also close companions of Ali and he when his wife was attending church with him and others he has come to know since she left to be with the Lord.

Paul's greatest earthly delight, however, and the one to which he devotes most of his time, is his position as manager of Team Watson.

Brian and Andrea Duff have continued to support him over the past two years as he has learnt, by experience, the skills of a father in family management. Since their daughter Molly is about the same age as Mark, Andrea often volunteers to take Mark and Euan to kids' activities in the Church, swimming lessons, birthday parties and the like.

It is on such occasions, either in a home or in a car, and when the children are unaware of an adult presence, when the most heartwarming, and often thought-provoking to adults but matter-of-fact to children, conversations are heard.

Paul finds the complete ease with which his boys, and especially Mark, can direct his friends to and then proceed to carry them through, a discussion on the subject of heaven, quite thrilling. This is not some theological theory to him. It is merely a simple fact.

He and Andrea have been eager but unobtrusive eavesdroppers to such deliberations a number of times over the period since Mark's mum took up the 'job God had for her to do.'

On one such time when Callum, another little boy from Glenabbey had joined them in the Duff home the conversation was most enlightening.

This time, and for a change, it was not Mark who brought up

the subject, but Callum.

"Mark, is your mummy sitting on a golden throne in Heaven?" he enquired, totally out of the blue.

Completely unfazed, Mark who considered himself something of an expert on the hereafter replied, without a moment's hesitation, "I don't know. Maybe she is walking on the golden streets."

Then Molly, not to be outdone chipped in, "Or maybe she is swimming in the golden sea!"

The truth is that speculation on what Ali is doing in heaven has to remain in the realm of childish conjecture.. Whether she happens to be sitting, walking or swimming is of no immediate consequence.

What is really important to Team Watson is that their best player is there, she is with Jesus, and in the words of Mark's memorable declaration, "Mummy's not sick anymore!"

If you have been helped or inspired by Ali's story or wish to comment on it we would love to hear from you.

alisbook@hotmail.co.uk

Email the author:
n.i.davidson@btinternet.com

Useful Websites:
www.glenabbey.co.uk
www.nihospicecare.com